FOCUS ON

FILM
AND THEATRE

◆◆◆

edited by

JAMES HURT

A SPECTRUM BOOK

Prentice-Hall, Inc.
Englewood Cliffs, N. J.

Library of Congress Cataloging in Publication Data

Hurt, James, comp.
  Focus on film and theatre.

  (Film focus) (A Spectrum Book)
    CONTENTS: Hurt, J. Introduction: Film/theatre/film
/theatre/film.—Critics: Lindsay, V. Thirty
differences between the photoplays and the stage.
Nicoll, A. Film reality: the cinema and the theatre.
Bentley, E. Realism and the cinema. Gilman, R. About
nothing—with precision. Kauffmann, S. Notes on
theatre-and-film. [etc.]
    1. Moving-pictures—Addresses, essays, lectures.
2. Theater—Addresses, essays, lectures. I. Title.
PN1995.H87   791.43   73–19523
ISBN 0–13–314666–9
ISBN 0–13–314658–8 (pbk.)

FILM FOCUS

Ronald Gottesman and Harry M. Geduld
General Editors

James Hurt, *editor of this volume,*
is Professor of English at the University of Illinois.

© 1974 by PRENTICE-HALL, INC.
Englewood Cliffs, New Jersey

A SPECTRUM BOOK

Printed in the United States of America
10 9 8 7 6 5 4 3 2 1

PRENTICE-HALL INTERNATIONAL, INC. (*London*)
PRENTICE-HALL OF AUSTRALIA, PTY. LTD. (*Sidney*)
PRENTICE-HALL OF CANADA, LTD. (*Toronto*)
PRENTICE-HALL OF INDIA PRIVATE LIMITED (*New Delhi*)
PRENTICE-HALL OF JAPAN, INC. (*Tokyo*)

CONTENTS

Introduction:

Film/Theatre/Film/Theatre/Film
by JAMES HURT

In 1918, Russian symbolist poet Alexander Blok wrote to a friend:

> I have nothing new now ready for the screen but I have more
> than once thought of writing for it: I always feel, however, that
> this will have to find a new technique for itself. In my opinion
> cinema has nothing in common with theatre, is not attached to
> it, does not compete with it, nor can they destroy each other;
> those once fashionable discussions on "cinema and theatre" seem
> quite unreal to me. I have long loved the cinema just as it was.[1]

Why, half a century later, are those "once fashionable discussions"
of film and theatre still going on so vigorously that it seems desirable to gather a few of the best and most representative of them into
a book? Over the seventy-five years that constitute the brief but
spectacular history of the movies, every major film critic, and a
number of literary and dramatic critics as well, have considered the
relationship of film and theatre. And the subject is far from exhausted; indeed, over the months that this volume was in preparation, a number of new treatments of the subject appeared and had
to be considered for inclusion.

The topic has proved to be so crucial and seemingly inexhaustible
for a number of reasons. One is that, though it has often been

[1] Quoted in Jay Leyda, *Kino: A History of the Russian and Soviet Film* (London: George Allen and Unwin, 1960), p. 130.

treated in rather abstract terms, it is by no means of merely theoretical interest. Ever since the day when the stage actor and writer D. W. Griffith walked over to the Edison studios in the Bronx and took a "temporary" job acting in the movies, actors, directors, and writers have found it important to be able to move freely between the stage, the movie studio, and now, the television studio. No theatre-trained actor can step before the camera for the first time without the question of the relationship and the differences between film and theatre taking on an urgent reality. And the question is similarly crucial for the playwright commissioned to turn his stage play into a shooting script, for the TV actor who has landed a summer stock job, and for the director who is offered a chance to make his first movie.

Another reason the topic is still alive is that, as Blok hoped, film "found a new technique for itself," and far from destroying each other, film and theatre have continued to evolve and develop each in its own way, sometimes diverging, sometimes converging, but always exercising a powerful and mutual influence upon each other. As they have mutated and evolved at the sometimes dizzying rate that has characterized twentieth-century art's "tradition of the new," it has been continually necessary to reconsider and reformulate critical descriptions of their relationship. A comparison of film and theatre written in the twenties, when film was mute and when the chief theatrical model was still the well-made play, must seem quaintly irrelevant in an age in which film is an auditory as well as a visual experience and in which the theatre-goer is less likely to find himself a voyeur peeping into a drawing room than a participant in a ritual, a ceremony, or an encounter-group session or the victim of a visual, auditory, and sometimes even personal assault.

Historically, each stage in the development of the film has raised new questions and has brought about fresh resolutions in the relationship of film to theatre. The history of primitive film, from the early 1890's to about 1915, for example, was marked by a gradual conquest of the theatrical audience and by the rapid development of a cinematic style clearly distinct from that of the theatre. A. Nicholas Vardac has voluminously documented the theatrical situation at the time the movies were born and the way in which the theatre created a "climate of acceptance" for them. The theatre of the late nineteenth century, both in Europe and America, was in reality two theatres. On the one hand, there was the flourishing but tiny serious art theatre, represented by the Théâtre Libre in Paris, the Freie Bühne in Berlin, J. T. Grein's Independent Theatre in London, and the Moscow Art Theatre, playing the established "classic" drama of Shakespeare, Goethe, etc., and the works of the late nine-teenth-century masters, Ibsen, Strindberg, and Chekhov, as well as the new social drama of such playwrights as Shaw and Brieux. On the other, there was the vast theatre of commodity entertainment which reached out from the cities to even the smallest villages with vaudeville, light comedy, and melodrama. The popular drama of the period was marked by an extreme rejection of realism in con-tent and by an equally extreme insistence upon it in presentation. A domestic drama might deal with stereotyped characters and plati-tudinous themes, but it was presented with a minute, "cup and saucer" realism. Or a melodrama might be pure escapism or wish fulfillment, but the details of its fantasizing were given the most lit-eral, concrete reality. The masters of this "pictorial realism" were Sir Henry Irving, Steele MacKaye, and David Belasco. In their theatres, ships could sink, locomotives could collide, and battles could be fought on stage with a breathtaking realism. As W. S. Gil-bert wryly observed, "Every play which contains a house on fire, a sinking steamer, a railway accident, and a dance in a casino, will (if it is liberally placed on the stage) succeed in spite of itself. In point of fact, nothing could wreck such a piece but carefully written dialogue and strict attention to probability." [2]

The movies took over this popular aesthetic almost immediately, and it was soon clear that they could easily surpass the theatre in spectacular realistic effects. One of the first productions for the Edison Kinetoscope, for example, was "The Execution of Mary, Queen of Scots" (1895), a filmstrip by William Heiss inspired by a popular stage treatment of the subject. Thanks to his ability to manipulate reality by stopping the camera, substituting a dummy,

[2] Quoted in J. O. Bailey, ed., *British Plays of the Nineteenth Century* (New York: Odyssey, 1966), p. 7.

and starting it again, Heiss was able to show the executioner's axe actually falling on Mary's neck and her head rolling off the block. The initial reaction of the theatre to such feats was to try to mount even more extraordinary spectacles, such as those in *Ben Hur* (1899), *The Light That Failed* (1903), and *Judith of Bethulia* (1904). But the battle was lost before it was begun, and the theatre had been forced to move in other directions even before D. W. Griffith's epic films of 1915–16, *Birth of a Nation* and *Intolerance,* signaled the film's triumph in the field of popular spectacle.

As film succeeded the theatre as the chief supplier of spectacular commodity entertainment, it captured the vast popular audience the theatre had commanded. In Europe, the shift was accelerated by the theatre's wartime difficulties just as imported American movies were becoming popular. The years 1915 to 1920 were marked by the wholesale conversion of legitimate theatres to movie houses, as the movies expanded into multimillion-dollar industries. The result, for the theatre, was a radical shift in the size and importance of the "two theatres." Since 1920, the popular theatre has been in decline, while the art theatre has maintained and even increased its prestige and influence, with a comparatively small elite audience.

During the years that the films were capturing the theatre's mass audience, they were developing a body of techniques more and more divergent from that of the theatre. The earliest film-makers used film strictly as a medium, to record either "found" real events or stage events (or what could easily have been stage events). In staged films, the camera remained fixed at what would have been third row center, actors entered and exited from the sides or the rear of a continuously visible space, and the action was arranged horizontally and pointed toward the camera-audience. Every film student recalls the excitement, in watching a well-selected survey of early films, of seeing the compressed development of a genuinely filmic idiom. From the filmed stage fantasies of Georges Méliès and the passive recordings of reality of the Lumière brothers through the innovations of Edwin S. Porter—shifts in the position of the camera, free manipulation of space and time, creation of a scene through the combination of a number of shots—to D. W. Griffith's refinement and consolidation of a full vocabulary of types of shots and of editing, lighting, and acting techniques, the movies within a decade and a half became an autonomous art, not merely a novelty or a medium for theatrical material.

As the movies "liberated" themselves from the stage, however, the theatre itself was rapidly evolving, often in ways influenced by the movies. The presence of the movies was continually felt throughout the vigorous theatrical experimentation of the twenties. The theatre was seeking a new area of activity the movies could not usurp; it also frequently tried to explore ways of imitating and incorporating film techniques. In France, Germany, Italy, and Russia, the theatrical avant-garde frequently expressed an admiration for the film's dreamlike fluidity, its power to convey subjective states, and its possibilities as a truly proletarian and antibourgeois art. In France, the Surrealist theatrical experiments of such writers as André Breton, Guillaume Apollinaire, Louis Aragon, and Antonin Artaud were perhaps better suited to the film than to the stage, assaulting as they did the theatre's traditional objectivity and its bondage to continuous time and space. And a number of Surrealists did indeed move from the theatre to the film, most notably Jean Cocteau. In Germany, film was one element among many of the influences that led to theatrical Expressionism, and German film and theatre freely borrowed from each other during the twenties. The debt to the stage of such films as *The Cabinet of Doctor Caligari* (1919) has often been noted, and to cite only one example, the characteristic roving spotlight of the Expressionist stage is an obvious attempt to control audience attention constantly in the manner of a film director. The attempts of the Bauhaus group to create a "total theatre" involved the incorporation of film into the total theatrical experience, as did the "Futurist Variety Theatre" conceived by Marinetti in Italy. The impact of film on the work of the most notable figure of the German theatre of the twenties—Bertolt Brecht—has never been fully explored, but it may have been a major influence on the cool, detached style, the directness of characterization, and the episodic plotting of the Epic Theatre. Brecht's ideas, of course, have had an enormous impact on both theatre directors and film-makers and would have been represented in this volume had it been possible to do justice to them in a short selection. The reader is referred to *Brecht on Theatre,* edited by John Willett (1964), for his major critical writings.

In Russia, where Lenin had declared that "of all the arts, the cinema is the most important for us," the twenties were filled with vigorous experiments in film and theatre, both separately and in combination. The productions of the Moscow Art Theatre were filmed, and the director, Vsevolod Meyerhold, called for a new theatre in which live and filmed scenes would be combined. The most famous product of this ferment, of course, is Sergei M. Eisenstein, whose entry into film was a logical step after his stage productions of 1923 had moved far in the direction of the realism and flexibility of the screen. "The cart dropped to pieces and its driver dropped into the cinema," as he wrote in the essay reprinted in this volume. It is sometimes forgotten, however, that he never abandoned his stage work, and his stage and film directing continued to influence each other throughout his life.

The lively and worldwide exploration of new forms in the film and in the theatre and their borrowings from each other in the 1920s left a permanent mark on both arts. Their relationship, however, was again abruptly changed in 1926–27 with the introduction of the sound film. The ultimate effect of this innovation was to complete the displacement of the theatre as a major purveyor of popular entertainment and to make the movies the dominant mass performance art for the next twenty years. Ironically, the initial effect, though, was to cancel out much of the film's hard-won stylistic autonomy and to bring about a marked "re-theatricalization" of film. In 1928 and 1929, playwrights, stage directors, and stage actors were imported en masse to teach the movies how to talk. Their theatrical orientation, plus the new technical problems presented by fixed microphones and cameras, using cumbersome "blimps" or suddenly caged in soundproof booths, resulted in a string of static, photographed stage musicals and revues, "all-talking and all-singing" though they might have been. The history of film in the 1930s was the history of the recovery of the technical mastery of the silent film, now applied to the sound film, through the work of the great directors of the period: Ernst Lubitsch, King Vidor, Rene Clair,

Jean Renoir, Rouben Mamoulian, John Ford, and many others, in the United States and abroad.

The movies' prosperous twenty years between 1930 and 1950 came to an end through two forces: the postwar court rulings that broke up the American corporate chains of studio-owned movie theatres, and the coming of television. The movies' response to television's challenge for the mass audience was remarkably similar to that of the popular theatre of half a century before, when the movies had been the challenger; it first tried to retain its audience through spectacle and gimmickry—3-D, Cinerama, CinemaScope, new color processes—but it finally accepted defeat, collaborating with the new medium, and at the same time, beginning to build new, minority audiences of its own.

The result of this revolution has been to place film in yet another relationship to theatre, both sociologically and artistically. Film has not been "re-theatricalized" as it was after the sound revolution of the twenties; on the contrary, it has tended to guard its integrity as film even more jealously. But economic and technological developments have forced it into a path more parallel to that of the theatre than ever before. Like the theatre, film has maintained its connections with popular entertainment, but like the theatre of the twenties, it has seen a sudden expansion and an increased importance in its minority audience. The result has, arguably, been a gain in some respects for film. For the first time in its history, serious ideas and feelings are as likely to find artistic expression in film as in the theatre. The makers of the theatre since 1950—Beckett, Ionesco, Genet, Osborne, Pinter—are equalled in stature and achievement by the makers of film—Bergman, Fellini, Antonioni, Truffaut, Godard, Kubrick. The richness, complexity, and subtlety of the best contemporary films perhaps results from the fact that serious filmmakers, like serious dramatists, no longer have to please everybody but can find an appropriate minority audience for their work.

The theoretical interrelationships of film and theatre are as complex as their historical ones, and indeed the historical development of each art and their reciprocal influence have made theoretical comparisons difficult and short-lived.

The gross similarities of film and theatre are obvious, though more critical attention has been devoted to their differences. Both are performance arts that ordinarily involve an audience gathering at a prescribed time in a theatre to witness a scheduled event (like dance and live music and unlike painting, sculpture, and novels). Both, traditionally at least, are narrative (they tell stories) and mimetic (they represent life). Furthermore, as we have seen, both are poised on a borderline between entertainment and art. Both suffer when they move too far from this line: the highest artistic achievement in both seems to require deep roots in popular convention.

The many contrasts that have been suggested between the two may be grouped along the old Aristotelian lines of creator, audience, and thing created. The question of who is the creator of a play and film has engaged a number of critics. In drama it is the playwright, in film it is the director, we are told, at least by the currently fashionable *"auteur"* film critics. And yet the proposition is far from conclusive. The supremacy of the playwright is an idea promulgated by literary critics, and if we regard drama in terms of performance, rather than text, the playwright assumes a role of *primus inter pares* with director and actors. On the other hand, the excesses of *auteur* criticism have led to a sometimes absurd overvaluation of the director's role in film-making: a director may occasionally make a good film out of a bad script, but this is probably rarer than the more extreme *auteur* critics would have us believe. In contemporary film and theatre, the traditional distinctions are further blurred by an increasing emphasis upon the film-script as a literary form (as in the work of Pinter, Beckett, Robbe-Grillet, etc.), and by the rise of something like *auteur*-directors in the theatre (Peter Brook, Jerzy Grotowski, Joseph Chaikin, etc.).

The contrast between film and theatre in audience and audience-experience is also a recurring subject in criticism, and one that might have been more fully represented in this collection. The idea that appears occasionally in early criticism—that the film audience is a mass audience, while the theatre audience is an elite, minority audience—is, as we have seen, a function of particular social and economic conditions and has nothing to do with the inherent properties of the two arts. More interesting are contrasts between modes of perceiving theatrical and cinematic performances. McLuhan's judgment that live theatre is a "cooler medium" than film—that is, that it requires more active participation from its audience —has been anticipated many times in film criticism. The ordinary circumstances of theatre-going make it a comparatively public event and discourage the dreamlike passivity which has been described as the film experience. In the theatre, the audience gathers in a group and waits for curtain time, the auditorium is more brightly lighted during the performance than a movie house is, and absorption in the drama is periodically broken by intermissions and scene changes. During the performance itself, the audience member must actively suspend his disbelief, since even the most realistic production requires the acceptance of a number of obvious conventions, and must actively participate in choosing what to look at, since the entire stage is ordinarily continuously in view. The movie audience, by contrast, is atomized, entering the theatre singly or in small groups and, even, at any point during the film. Isolated in the darkness and staring at a screen much more commanding in size and brightness than the theatre stage, the movie-goer is much more likely to surrender control of his consciousness. It is comparatively easy to suspend disbelief since he is in the presence of a relatively exact representation of reality and he is asked to make a minimal number of choices in selecting what to look at, since he can see only what the film-maker shows him. He is relieved of even the minimal tension which invariably accompanies performances by live actors, with the continual possibility of human error—blown lines and other misadventures.

There is still a great deal of truth in these often-repeated observations, but perhaps less now than in an age when the movies were frankly escapist entertainment and the theatre was dominated by the realistic style. Films no more than other serious art forms seek merely to suck us up into mindless, wish fulfillment fantasies. The Brechtian revolution has reached the screen as well as the stage, and contemporary films are full of distancing devices, implicit as well as explicit, from the frank metacinematic devices of *Tom Jones* or *Persona* to the cool, terse, antifantasizing tone of such films as those of Godard. At the same time, much contemporary theatre—especially that ultimately derived from the ideas of Artaud—seeks to achieve the kind of visceral, irrational involvement sometimes associated with the movies. The goal is hardly cool, detached observation in such productions as Peter Brook's *Marat/Sade* or those of the Living Theatre or the Polish Laboratory Theatre.

More numerous than studies of creator or audience, however, have been studies of the object itself: the film and the play. Some critics have made an initial contrast that even denies that they are comparable, since a film is literally an object and theatre is an event. But surely the essential film is not the celluloid in the can (any more than a play is pages in a book), but rather the showing of the film—a performance-event also. There are of course a number of sharp contrasts between theatre and film as performance: theatre is three-dimensional, film is two-dimensional; in the theatre we see a performance being created as we watch it, in film we never quite forget that we are seeing a record of a performance that has taken place in the past; actors' performances vary from night to night in the theatre, they are fixed in film; performance and role are generally distinct in the theatre, in film they are generally synonymous. Many other contrasts could be listed (most of them open to exceptions and qualifications), but we may concentrate on three areas that have stimulated most discussion: time, space, and structure.

One of the most liberating insights in the early development of film technique was that the film need not be bound to the theatre's use of continuous and sequential time. On the stage, as Stanley Kauffmann points out in the essay reprinted in this volume, an actor crossing a room has to cross it step by step; in the film, he can come in at the door and immediately be at the other side of the room. The film has great flexibility in thus eliding time, presenting simultaneous action, leaping back and forth among past, present, and future, and repeating moments over and over. This flexibility is generally represented as a strength of film, which of course it is, but the theatre's ways of representing time are not therefore a weakness. The theatre, in the first place, is not so inflexible in its representation of time as is sometimes implied: in *Agamemnon*, for example,

Aeschylus uses a time ellipsis in representing the time between the fall of Troy and the arrival of Agamemnon's army, Shakespeare often uses a flexible "stage time" which compresses, lengthens, or otherwise distorts "real time," and modern plays often treat time almost as fluidly as film does: the second half of Brecht's *Caucasian Chalk Circle,* for example, begins at the same point in time as the first half, and Jean-Claude Van Itallie has written a number of plays that play games with instantaneous action, repetitions, time loops, and other distortions. In the second place, the theatre's more characteristic representation of time as a steady, sequential unfolding is one of its great strengths, as the Greeks and Ibsen showed us in the past and as such modern plays as Albee's *Who's Afraid of Virginia Woolf?* and Pinter's *The Homecoming* have demonstrated once again.

The contrast between the theatrical and cinematic representation of space is much like the contrast in the representation of time. Theatre is confined to a continuous use of stage space (though the stage space may constitute a figurative treatment of real space, as stage time may constitute a figurative treatment of real time). Film can treat space as flexibly and fluidly as it can treat time, moving freely back and forth over any spatial expanse. The sharpest contrast, however, is in the spatial relationship of the spectator to the action. In the theatre, the spectator ordinarily is fixed in one position, viewing the action from a constant position and point of view. In the film, the spectator, though he remains physically in his seat, is perceptually constantly changing his perspective, moving in upon the action, moving back from it, seeing it from the position of one of the characters, or even from a position impossible in real experience (as in *Potemkin,* for example, when we see the mutiny from high above the ship). Again, however, the fact that the film's use of space is a great strength does not mean that the theatre's use of it is a weakness. As Kauffmann points out, the cliché that a play benefits by being "opened up" spatially when it becomes a film betrays a fundamental lack of understanding of the way a good play builds vertically while a good film builds laterally. Stage space is invariably metaphorical, even when it is most "realistic," and one of the great strengths of drama is its power to charge a confined space with emotional meaning. "Opening up" a play is usually desirable, but it must be a part of a total rethinking of the way space is to be used in the new medium. (See, for example, Elia Kazan's comments in this volume on his experiences in adapting *A Streetcar Named Desire* for the screen.)

Closely related to the use of time and space is the question of structure in film and theatre. The film's freedom from the theatrical constraints of continuous time and space make the shot the fundamental unit of film structure. The shot is thus comparable, not to the theatrical scene, as is sometimes said, but to the theatrical "beat," the introduction and resolution of a conflict of wills which constitutes the minimal unit of drama. Theatrical scenes are built up out of these minimal units as cinematic scenes are built up out of series of shots. The comparison cannot be pushed further, however, since shots are defined by visual considerations—distance, point of view, movement—while beats are defined psychologically, as "units of conflict." Thus at the most elementary level, film is "seeing" while drama is "interacting." The intermediate structures of drama—the patterns which organize larger units such as scenes and acts—are generally public or private rituals: trials, weddings, funerals, arrivals, departures, confrontations, conversations, and the like. It is the nature of the rituals employed in these intermediate structures which largely defines dramatic style, from the public and ceremonial style of the Greeks to the closeted and domestic style of the modern realists. The intermediate structures of film are ordinarily much looser and less ritualistic: they tend to organize material along perceptual lines, as the eye would perceive it, rather than along the lines of formal human interaction. The heavy use of the kinds of intermediate structures used in drama tends to give films a theatrical flavor, as in, say, Renoir's *Rules of the Game*. A similar contrast between the natural structures of film and theatre seems to exist for the largest units. Perhaps because of the film's much closer ties to surface reality—the appearance of things—it often seems that a film begins in the concrete and moves toward an organizing idea while a play begins with an idea and moves toward its concrete embodiment. Whether or not this is literally true, it does seem that the greatest drama tends in its largest patterns to-ward the mythic and the archetypal, while even the greatest films cannot move very far from the confusion of immediate reality with-out appearing "stagy" and "literary." Thus the essence of many fine and complex plays can often be suggested in a short summary of their basic action; the essence of a fine movie can rarely be cap-tured so simply.

The difficulty in selecting the contents of this collection has been in choosing from a vast amount of material, since, so closely have film and theatre been intertwined, almost everything that has been written on film touches, at least implicitly, on the theatrical com-parison. I have tried to select material that suggests the range of the subject, both in time and in point of view.

The five essays that make up the first half of the book represent the views of critics over practically the entire history of the movies. Vachel Lindsay, best known as a poet, was also an enthusiast of the movies and one of their best early critics in *The Art of the Mov-ing Picture* (1916), from which the present selection is taken. Lind-say's shrewd analysis of "thirty differences" between the two arts is not only of historical interest, but also has considerable validity to-day, despite the passage of sixty-five years of cinematic and dramatic history. (I must confess, however, that I still do not know what the "thirty differences" are; I get a different number each time I count.)

Allardyce Nicoll's "Film Reality: The Cinema and the Theatre" is a key chapter from his important book *Film and Theatre* (1937), which has influenced most subsequent writers on the subject. The section from Eric Bentley's *The Playwright as Thinker* (1946) is a friendly reply to one of Nicoll's central points—that "the film has such a hold over the world of reality . . . that the realistic play must surely come to seem trivial, false, and inconsequential" and that therefore the theatre should move in the direction of artifice.

Richard Gilman's "About Nothing—with Precision" (1962) sur-veys the situation sixteen years after Bentley wrote so optimistically about the future of theatrical realism. Gilman, a critic who moves freely between film and theatre, finds the theatre artistically bank-rupt, its only hope resting in a few plays which employ "new lan-

guages" to break with the theater's "consecration of what has ceased
to exist." Its place has been taken by movies: "true shadows" which
are replacing "unreal actuality."

Stanley Kauffmann's "Notes on Theatre-and-Film" (1972) appeared while this volume was in preparation. His shrewd, sensible,
and ironic debunking of some widely accepted dogmas on the subject seemed a perfect conclusion to the critical section of the collection.

The second half of the book turns from the theoretical and critical emphasis of the first half to the reflections and comments of
those who practice the two arts: actors, directors, and playwrights.
Josef von Sternberg's urbane and witty "Acting in Film and Theatre"
(1955) reflects the experience of a director famous for his work with
actors, most notably Marlene Dietrich. "The Player: Actors Talk
About Film Acting" is a selection from Lillian Ross and Helen
Ross's *The Player: A Profile of an Art* (1962), a collection of interviews with actors remarkably free from cant and press-agentry. In
these selections, twelve prominent actors comment on their experiences in moving back and forth between the two media.

The next two essays present the views of two prominent directors
from two eras in film. In "Through Theatre to Cinema" (1934),
Sergei Eisenstein describes how even in his stage directing in the
early twenties, he was moving toward cinematic techniques. The
interview with Elia Kazan offers a detailed account of the experiences of one of the few men who is a major director in both media,
as well as a novelist and screen-writer.

The last section brings together three playwrights widely separated in time and style. Shaw was the first major playwright of the
film era, and he had as strong opinions on the film as on most other
things. The conversation with Archibald Henderson reprinted here
from *Table-Talk* (1925) preceded most of Shaw's direct contacts
with film-making; his later experiences are well described in Donald P. Costello's *The Serpent's Eye: Shaw and the Cinema* (1965).
Harold Pinter, one of the two or three most prominent living playwrights, has moved freely between theatre and film in a series of
stunning plays and almost equally impressive screenplays. In the in-

terview reprinted here, Pinter and his director, Clive Donner, describe how they turned *The Caretaker* into a film.

The final selection looks to the future; it is an essay by the brilliant and iconoclastic young Austrian playwright and critic, Peter Handke. In this witty essay, Handke attacks currently prestigious "art" films and plays and calls for a new kind of film in which the "syntax" of the film becomes the film itself and for an equally self-referring new theatre of actual events.

Perhaps the best indication that a collection of essays on the subject of film and theatre is worthwhile at this point in time is the certainty that it will before long become obsolete. The subject is very much alive because film and theatre are so much alive, and it is well to pause and survey the terrain behind as we prepare to try to understand the new forms and relationships that seem certain to appear in the next few years.

CRITICS

Thirty Differences Between the Photoplays and the Stage
by VACHEL LINDSAY

The stage is dependent upon three lines of tradition: first, that of Greece and Rome that came down through the French. Second, the English style, ripened from the miracle play and the Shakespearian stage. And third, the Ibsen precedent from Norway, now so firmly established it is classic. These methods are obscured by the commercialized dramas, but they are behind them all. Let us discuss for illustration the Ibsen tradition.

Ibsen is generally the vitriolic foe of pageant. He must be read aloud. He stands for the spoken word, for the iron power of life that may be concentrated in a phrase like the "All or nothing" of Brand. Though Peer Gynt has its spectacular side, Ibsen generally comes in through the ear alone. He can be acted in essentials from end to end with one table and four chairs in any parlor. The alleged punch with which the "movie" culminates has occurred three or ten years before the Ibsen curtain goes up. At the close of every act of the dramas of this Norwegian one might inscribe on the curtain "This the magnificent moving picture cannot achieve." Likewise after every successful film described in this book could be inscribed "This the trenchant Ibsen cannot do."

But a photoplay of Ghosts came to our town. The humor of the prospect was the sort too deep for tears. My pastor and I reread the William Archer translation that we might be alert for every antithesis. Together we went to the services. Since then the film has been furiously denounced by the literati. Floyd Dell's discriminating assault upon it is quoted in Current Opinion, October, 1915, and Margaret Anderson prints a denunciation of it in a recent number of The Little Review. But it is not such a bad film in itself. It is not Ibsen. It should be advertised "The Iniquities of the Fathers, an American drama of Eugenics, in a Palatial Setting."

Henry Walthall as Alving, afterward as his son, shows the men much as Ibsen outlines their characters. Of course the only way to be Ibsen is to be so precisely. In the new plot all is open as the day. The world is welcome, and generally present when the man or his son go forth to see the elephant and hear the owl. Provincial hypocrisy is not implied. But Ibsen can scarcely exist without an atmosphere of secrecy for his human volcanoes to burst through in the end.

Mary Alden as Mrs. Alving shows in her intelligent and sensitive countenance that she has a conception of that character. She does not always have the chance to act the woman written in her face, the tart, thinking, handsome creature that Ibsen prefers. Nigel Debrullier looks the buttoned-up Pastor Manders, even to caricature. But the crawling, bootlicking carpenter, Jacob Engstrand, is changed into a respectable, guileless man with an income. And his wife and daughter are helpless, conventional, upper-class rabbits. They do not remind one of the saucy originals.

The original Ibsen drama is the result of mixing up five particular characters through three acts. There is not a situation but would go to pieces if one personality were altered. Here are two, sadly tampered with: Engstrand and his daughter. Here is the mother, who is only referred to in Ibsen. Here is the elder Alving, who disappears before the original play starts. So the twenty great Ibsen situations in the stage production are gone. One new crisis has an Ibsen irony and psychic tension. The boy is taken with the dreaded intermittent pains in the back of his head. He is painting the order that is to make him famous: the King's portrait. While the room empties of people he writhes on the floor. If this were all, it would have been one more moving picture failure to put through a tragic scene. But the thing is reiterated in tableau-symbol. He is looking sideways in terror. A hairy arm with clutching demon claws comes thrusting in toward the back of his neck. He writhes in deadly fear. The audience is appalled for him.

This visible clutch of heredity is the nearest equivalent that is offered for the whispered refrain: "Ghosts," in the original masterpiece. This hand should also be reiterated as a refrain, three times at least, before this tableau, each time more dreadful and threatening. It appears but the once, and has no chance to become a part of the accepted hieroglyphics of the piece, as it should be, to realize its full power.

The father's previous sins have been acted out. The boy's consequent struggle with the malady has been traced step by step, so the play should end here. It would then be a rough equivalent of the Ibsen irony in a contrary medium. Instead of that, it wanders on through paraphrases of scraps of the play, sometimes literal, then quite alien, on to the alleged motion picture punch, when the Doctor is the god from the machine. There is no doctor on the stage in the original Ghosts. But there is a physician in the Doll's House, a scientific, quietly moving oracle, crisp, Spartan, sophisticated.

Is this photoplay physician such a one? The boy and his half-sister are in their wedding-clothes in the big church. Pastor Manders is saying the ceremony. The audience and building are indeed showy. The doctor charges up the aisle at the moment people are told to speak or forever hold their peace. He has tact. He simply breaks up the marriage right there. He does not tell the guests why. But he takes the wedding party into the pastor's study and there blazes at the bride and groom the long-suppressed truth that they are brother and sister. Always an orotund man, he has the Chautauqua manner indeed in this exigency.

He brings to one's mind the tearful book, much loved in childhood, Parted at the Altar, or Why Was it Thus? And four able actors have the task of telling the audience by facial expression only, that they have been struck by moral lightning. They stand in a row, facing the people, endeavoring to make the crisis of an alleged Ibsen play out of a crashing melodrama.

The final death of young Alving is depicted with an approximation of Ibsen's mood. But the only ways to suggest such feelings in silence, do not convey them in full to the audience, but merely narrate them. Wherever in Ghosts we have quiet voices that are like the slow drip of hydrochloric acid, in the photoplay we have no quiet gestures that will do trenchant work. Instead there are endless writhings and rushings about, done with a deal of skill, but destructive of the last remnants of Ibsen.

Up past the point of the clutching hand this film is the prime example for study for the person who would know once for all the differences between the photoplays and the stage dramas. Along with it might be classed Mrs. Fiske's decorative moving picture Tess, in which there is every determination to convey the original Mrs. Fiske illusion without her voice and breathing presence. To people who know her well it is a surprisingly good tintype of our beloved friend, for the family album. The relentless Thomas Hardy is nowhere to be found. There are two moments of dramatic life set among many of delicious pictorial quality: when Tess baptizes her child, and when she smooths its little grave with a wavering hand. But in the stage-version the dramatic poignancy begins with the going up of the curtain, and lasts till it descends.

The prime example of complete failure is Sarah Bernhardt's Camille. It is indeed a tintype of the consumptive heroine, with every group entire, and taken at full length. Much space is occupied by the floor and the overhead portions of the stage setting. It lasts as long as would the spoken performance, and wherever there is a dialogue we must imagine said conversation if we can. It might be compared to watching Camille from the top gallery through smoked glass, with one's ears stopped with cotton.

It would be well for the beginning student to find some way to see the first two of these three, or some other attempts to revamp the classic, for instance Mrs. Fiske's painstaking reproduction of Vanity Fair, bearing in mind the list of differences which this chapter now furnishes.

There is no denying that many stage managers who have taken up photoplays are struggling with the Shakespearian French and Norwegian traditions in the new medium. Many of the moving pictures discussed in this book are rewritten stage dramas, and one, Judith of Bethulia, is a pronounced success. But in order to be real photoplays the stage dramas must be overhauled indeed, turned inside out and upside down. The successful motion picture expresses itself through mechanical devices that are being evolved every hour. Upon those many new bits of machinery are founded novel methods of combination in another field of logic, not dramatic logic, but tableau logic. But the old-line managers, taking up photoplays, begin by making curious miniatures of stage presentations. They try to have most things as before. Later they take on the moving picture technique in a superficial way, but they, and the host of talented actors in the prime of life and Broadway success, retain the dramatic state of mind.

It is a principle of criticism, the world over, that the distinctions between the arts must be clearly marked, even by those who afterwards mix those arts. Take, for instance, the perpetual quarrel between the artists and the half-educated about literary painting. Whistler fought that battle in England. He tried to beat it into the head of John Bull that a painting is one thing, a mere illustration for a story another thing. But the novice is always stubborn. To him Hindu and Arabic are both foreign languages, therefore just alike. The book illustration may be said to come in through the ear, by reading the title aloud in imagination. And the other is effective with no title at all. The scenario writer who will study to the bottom of the matter in Whistler's Gentle Art of Making Enemies will be equipped to welcome the distinction between the old-fashioned stage, where the word rules, and the photoplay, where splendor and ritual are all. It is not the same distinction, but a kindred one.

But let us consider the details of the matter. The stage has its exits and entrances at the side and back. The standard photoplays have their exits and entrances across the imaginary footlight line, even in the most stirring mob and battle scenes. In Judith of Bethu-

lia, though the people seem to be coming from everywhere and going everywhere, when we watch close, we see that the individuals
enter at the near right-hand corner and exit at the near left-hand
corner, or enter at the near left-hand corner and exit at the near
right-hand corner.

Consider the devices whereby the stage actor holds the audience
as he goes out at the side and back. He sighs, gestures, howls, and
strides. With what studious preparation he ripens his quietness, if
he goes out that way. In the new contraption, the moving picture,
the hero or villain in exit strides past the nose of the camera, growing much bigger than a human being, marching toward us as
though he would step on our heads, disappearing when largest.
There is an explosive power about the mildest motion picture exit,
be the actor skilful or the reverse. The people left in the scene are
pygmies compared with each disappearing cyclops. Likewise, when
the actor enters again, his mechanical importance is overwhelming.
Therefore, for his first entrance the motion picture star does not
require the preparations that are made on the stage. The support
does not need to warm the spectators to the problem, then talk them
into surrender.

When the veteran stage-producer as a beginning photoplay producer tries to give us a dialogue in the motion pictures, he makes
it so dull no one follows. He does not realize that his camera-born
opportunity to magnify persons and things instantly, to interweave
them as actors on one level, to alternate scenes at the slightest whim,
are the big substitutes for dialogue. By alternating scenes rapidly,
flash after flash: cottage, field, mountain-top, field, mountain-top,
cottage, we have a conversation between three places rather than
three persons. By alternating the picture of a man and the check
he is forging, we have his soliloquy. When two people talk to each
other, it is by lifting and lowering objects rather than their voices.
The collector presents a bill: the adventurer shows him the door.
The boy plucks a rose: the girl accepts it. Moving objects, not moving lips, make the words of the photoplay.

The old-fashioned stage producer, feeling he is getting nowhere,
but still helpless, puts the climax of some puzzling lip-debate, often
the climax of the whole film, as a sentence on the screen. Sentences

should be used to show changes of time and place and a few such elementary matters before the episode is fully started. The climax of a motion picture scene cannot be one word or fifty words. As has been discussed in connection with Cabiria, the crisis must be an action sharper than any that has gone before in organic union with a tableau more beautiful than any that has preceded: the breaking of the tenth wave upon the sand. Such remnants of pantomimic dialogue as remain in the main chase of the photoplay film are but guide-posts in the race toward the goal. They should not be elaborate toll-gates of plot, to be laboriously lifted and lowered while the horses stop, mid-career.

The Venus of Milo, that comes directly to the soul through the silence, requires no quotation from Keats to explain her, though Keats is the equivalent in verse. Her setting in the great French Museum is enough. We do not know that her name is Venus. She is thought by many to be another statue of Victory. We may some day evolve scenarios that will require nothing more than a title thrown upon the screen at the beginning, they come to the eye so perfectly. This is not the only possible sort, but the self-imposed limitation in certain films might give them a charm akin to that of the Songs without Words.

The stage audience is a unit of three hundred or a thousand. In the beginning of the first act there is much moving about and extra talk on the part of the actors, to hold the crowd while it is settling down, and enable the late-comer to be in his seat before the vital part of the story starts. If he appears later, he is glared at. In the motion picture art gallery, on the other hand, the audience is around two hundred, and these are not a unit, and the only crime is to obstruct the line of vision. The high-school girls can do a moderate amount of giggling without breaking the spell. There is no spell, in the stage sense, to break. People can climb over each other's knees to get in or out. If the picture is political, they murmur war-cries to one another. If the film suggests what some of the neighbors have been doing, they can regale each other with the richest sewing society report.

The people in the motion picture audience total about two hundred, any time, but they come in groups of two or three at no specified hour. The newcomers do not, as in Vaudeville, make themselves part of a jocular army. Strictly as individuals they judge the panorama. If they disapprove, there is grumbling under their breath, but no hissing. I have never heard an audience in a photoplay theatre clap its hands even when the house was bursting with people. Yet they often see the film through twice. When they have had enough, they stroll home. They manifest their favorable verdict by sending some other member of the family to "see the picture." If the people so delegated are likewise satisfied, they may ask the man at the door if he is going to bring it back. That is the moving picture kind of cheering.

It was a theatrical sin when the old-fashioned stage actor was rendered unimportant by his scenery. But the motion picture actor is but the mood of the mob or the landscape or the department store behind him, reduced to a single hieroglyphic.

The stage-interior is large. The motion-picture interior is small. The stage out-of-door scene is at best artificial and little and is generally at rest, or its movement is tainted with artificiality. The waves dash, but not dashingly, the water flows, but not flowingly. The motion picture out-of-door scene is as big as the universe. And only pictures of the Sahara are without magnificent motion.

The photoplay is as far from the stage on the one hand as it is from the novel on the other. Its nearest analogy in literature is, perhaps, the short story, or the lyric poem. The key-words of the stage are *passion* and *character;* of the photoplay, *splendor* and *speed.* The stage in its greatest power deals with pity for some one especially unfortunate, with whom we grow well acquainted; with some private revenge against some particular despoiler; traces the beginning and culmination of joy based on the gratification of some preference, or love for some person, whose charm is all his own. The drama is concerned with the slow, inevitable approaches to these intensities. On the other hand, the motion picture, though often appearing to deal with these things, as a matter of fact uses substitutes, many of which have been listed. But to review: its first substitute is the excitement of speed-mania stretched on the framework of an obvious plot. Or it deals with delicate informal anecdote as the short story does, or fairy legerdemain, or patriotic ban-

ners, or great surging mobs of the proletariat, or big scenic out-
looks, or miraculous beings made visible. And the further it gets
from Euripides, Ibsen, Shakespeare, or Molière—the more it becomes like a mural painting from which flashes of lightning come
—the more it realizes its genius. Men like Gordon Craig and Gran-
ville Barker are almost wasting their genius on the theatre. The
Splendor Photoplays are the great outlet for their type of imagination.

The typical stage performance is from two hours and a half upward. The movie show generally lasts five reels, that is, an hour and
forty minutes. And it should last but three reels, that is, an hour.
Edgar Poe said there was no such thing as a long poem. There is
certainly no such thing as a long moving picture masterpiece.

The stage-production depends most largely upon the power of
the actors, the movie show upon the genius of the producer. The
performers and the dumb objects are on equal terms in his paint-
buckets. The star-system is bad for the stage because the minor
parts are smothered and the situations distorted to give the favorite
an orbit. It is bad for the motion pictures because it obscures the
producer. While the leading actor is entitled to his glory, as are
all the actors, their mannerisms should not overshadow the latest
inspirations of the creator of the films.

The display of the name of the corporation is no substitute for
giving the glory to the producer. An artistic photoplay is not the
result of a military efficiency system. It is not a factory-made staple
article, but the product of the creative force of one soul, the flower-
ing of a spirit that has the habit of perpetually renewing itself.

Once I saw Mary Fuller in a classic. It was the life and death of
Mary Queen of Scots. Not only was the tense, fidgety, over-Ameri-
can Mary Fuller transformed into a being who was a poppy and a
tiger-lily and a snow-queen and a rose, but she and her company,
including Marc Macdemott, radiated the old Scotch patriotism.
They made the picture a memorial. It reminded one of Maurice
Hewlett's novel The Queen's Quair. Evidently all the actors were
fused by some noble managerial mood.

There can be no doubt that so able a group have evolved many
good films that have escaped me. But though I did go again and

again, never did I see them act with the same deliberation and distinction, and I laid the difference to a change in the state of mind of the producer. Even baseball players must have managers. A team cannot pick itself, or it surely would. And this rule may apply to the stage. But by comparison to motion picture performers, stage-actors are their own managers, for they have an approximate notion of how they look in the eye of the audience, which is but the human eye. They can hear and gauge their own voices. They have the same ears as their listeners. But the picture producer holds to his eyes the seven-leagued demon spy-glass called the kinetoscope, as the audience will do later. The actors have not the least notion of their appearance. Also the words in the motion picture are not things whose force the actor can gauge. The book under the table is one word, the dog behind the chair is another, the window curtain flying in the breeze is another.

This chapter has implied that the performers were but paint on the canvas. They are both paint and models. They are models in the sense that the young Ellen Terry was the inspiration for Watts' Sir Galahad. They resemble the persons in private life who furnish the basis for novels. Dickens' mother was the original of Mrs. Nickleby. His father entered into Wilkins Micawber. But these people are not perpetually thrust upon us as Mr. and Mrs. Dickens. We are glad to find them in the Dickens biographies. When the stories begin, it is Micawber and Mrs. Nickleby we want, and the Charles Dickens atmosphere.

The photoplays of the future will be written from the foundations for the films. The soundest actors, photographers, and producers will be those who emphasize the points wherein the photoplay is unique. What is adapted to complete expression in one art generally secures but half expression in another. The supreme photoplay will give us things that have been but half expressed in all other mediums allied to it.

Once this principle is grasped there is every reason why the same people who have interested themselves in the advanced experimental drama should take hold of the super-photoplay. The good citizens who can most easily grasp the distinction should be there to perpetuate the higher welfare of these institutions side by side.

This parallel development should come, if for no other reason, because the two arts are still roughly classed together by the public. The elect cannot teach the public what the drama is till they show them precisely what the photoplay is and is not. Just as the university has departments of both History and English teaching in amity, each one illuminating the work of the other, so these two forms should live in each other's sight in fine and friendly contrast. At present they are in blind and jealous warfare.

Film Reality: The Cinema
and the Theatre
by ALLARDYCE NICOLL

One question of fundamental importance remains for consideration. When we witness a film, do we anticipate something we should
not expect from a stage performance, and, if so, what effect has this
upon our appreciation of film acting? At first, we might be tempted
to dismiss such a query or to answer it easily and glibly. There is
no essential difference, we might say, save in so far as we expect
greater variety and movement on the screen than we do on the
stage; and for acting, that, we might reply, is obviously the same
as stage acting although perhaps more stabilised in type form. Do
we not see Charles Laughton, Cedric Hardwicke, Ernest Thesiger,
Elizabeth Bergner now in the theatre, now in the cinema? To consider further, we might say, were simply to indulge in useless and
uncalled for speculation.

Nevertheless, the question does demand just a trifle more of investigation. Some few years ago a British producing company made
a film of Bernard Shaw's *Arms and the Man*. This film, after a few
exciting shots depicting the dark streets of a Balkan town, the
frenzied flight of the miserable fugitives and the clambering of
Bluntschli onto Raina's window terrace, settled down to provide
what was fundamentally a screen-picture of the written drama. The
dialogue was shortened, no doubt, but the shots proceeded more

From Film and Theatre, *by Allardyce Nicoll. Copyright © 1964 by
Allardyce Nicoll. Reprinted by permission of Allardyce Nicoll.*

or less along the dramatic lines established by Shaw and nothing was introduced which he had not originally conceived in preparing his material for the stage. The result was that no more dismal film has ever been shown to the public. On the stage *Arms and the Man* is witty, provocative, incisively stimulating; its characters have a breath of genuine theatrical life; it moves, it breathes, it has vital energy. In the screen version all that life has fled, and, strangest thing of all, those characters—Bluntschli, Raina, Sergius—who are so exciting on the boards, looked to the audience like a set of wooden dummies, hopelessly patterned. Performed by a third-rate amateur cast their life-blood does not so ebb from them, yet here, interpreted by a group of distinguished professionals, they wilted and died—died, too, in such forms that we could never have credited them with ever having had a spark of reality. Was there any basic reason for this failure?

THE CAMERA'S TRUTH

The basic reason seems to be simply this—that practically all effectively drawn stage characters are types and that in the cinema we demand individualisation, or else that we recognise stage figures as types and impute greater power of independent life to the figures we see on the screen. This judgment, running so absolutely counter to what would have been our first answer to the original question posited, may seem grossly distorted, but perhaps some further consideration will demonstrate its plausibility. When we go to the theatre, we expect theatre and nothing else. We know that the building we enter is a playhouse; that behind the lowered curtain actors are making ready, dressing themselves in strange garments and transforming their natural features; that the figures we later see on the boards are never living persons of king and bishop and clown, but merely men pretending for a brief space of time to be like these figures. Dramatic illusion is never (or so rarely as to be negligible) the illusion of reality: it is always imaginative illusion, the illusion of a period of make-believe. All the time we watch Hamlet's throes of agony we know that the character Hamlet is being impersonated by a man who presently will walk out of the stage-door in ordinary clothes and an autograph-signing smile on his face. True, volumes have been written on famous dramatic characters—Greek, Elizabethan English and modern Norwegian—and these volumes might well seem to give the lie to such assumptions. Have not Shakespeare's characters seemed so real to a few observers that we have on our shelves books specifically concerned with the girlhood of his heroines—a girlhood the dramas themselves denied us?

These studies, however, should not distract us from the essential truth that the greatest playwrights have always aimed at presenting human personality in bold theatric terms. Hamlet seizes on us, not because he is an individual, not because in him Shakespeare has delineated a particular prince of Denmark, but because in Hamlet there are bits of all men; he is a composite character whose lineaments are determined by dramatic necessity, and through that he lives. Fundamentally, the truly vital theatre deals in stock figures. Like a child's box of bricks, the stage's material is limited; it is the possibilities in arrangement that are well-nigh inexhaustible. Audiences thrill to see new situations born of fresh sociological conditions, but the figures set before them in significant plays are conventionally fixed and familiar. Of Romeos there are many, and of Othellos legion. Character on the stage is restricted and stereotyped and the persons who play upon the boards are governed, not by the strangely perplexing processes of life but by the established terms of stage practice. Bluntschli represents half a hundred similar rationalists; the idealism of thousands is incorporated in Sergius; and Raina is an eternal stage type of the perplexing feminine. The theatre is populated, not by real individuals whose boyhood or girlhood may legitimately be traced, but by heroes and villains sprung full-bodied from Jove's brain, by clowns and pantaloons whose youth is unknown and whose future matters not after the curtain's fall.

In the cinema we demand something different. Probably we carry into the picture-house prejudices deeply ingrained in our beings. The statement that "the camera cannot lie" has been disproved by millions of flattering portraits and by dozens of spiritualistic pictures which purport to depict fairies but which mostly turn out to be faintly disguised pictures of ballet-dancers or replicas of figures in advertisements of night-lights. Yet in our heart of hearts we credit the truth of that statement. A picture, a piece of sculpture, a stage-play—these we know were created by man; we have watched the scenery being carried in back stage and we know we shall see the actors, turned into themselves again, bowing at the conclusion of the performance. In every way the "falsity" of a theatrical production is borne in upon us so that we are prepared to demand nothing save a theatrical truth. For the films, however, our orientation is vastly different. Several periodicals, it is true, have endeavored to let us into the secrets of the moving-picture industry and a few favored spectators have been permitted to make the rounds of the studios; but from ninety per cent of the audience the actual methods employed in the preparation of a film remain far off and dimly realised. "New York," we are told,

> struts when it constructs a Rockefeller Center. A small town chirps when it finishes a block of fine cottages. The government gets into the newspapers for projects like Boulder Dam. It takes Hollywood approximately three days to build Rome and a morning to effect its fall, but there is very little hurrah about it. The details are guarded like Victorian virtue.
>
> There is sound reticence on the part of a community that is usually articulate about its successes. Hollywood is in the business of building illusion, not sets. . . . The public likes to feel that the stork brought *The Birth of a Nation*. It likes to feel that a cameraman hung in the clouds—mid-Pacific—the day that Barrymore fought the whale.

That audience, accordingly, carries its prejudices with it intact. "The camera cannot lie"—and therefore, even when we are looking at Marlene Dietrich or Robert Montgomery, we unconsciously lose sight of fictional surroundings and interpret their impersonations as "real" things. Rudolph Valentino became a man who had had innumerable Sheikish adventures, and into each part she took the personality of Greta Garbo was incorporated. The most impossible actions may be shown us in a film, yet Laurel and Hardy are, at their best, seen as individuals experiencing many strange adventures, not as virtuoso comedians in a vaudeville act.

How true this is was demonstrated by a film, *Once in a Blue Moon,* which has been shown only in a few theatres. The general tone of *Once in a Blue Moon* was burlesque. In it was a "take-off" of certain Russian films, incidental jibes at a few popular American examples, and occasional skits directed at prominent players; Jimmy Savo took the rôle of Gabbo the Great while one of the actresses made up to look like Katherine Hepburn. The result was dismal. In Charlie Chaplin's free fantasy there is life and interest; throughout the course of *Once in a Blue Moon* vitality was entirely lacking. Nor was the reason far to seek. We cannot appreciate burlesque in the cinema because of the fact that in serious films actor and rôle are indistinguishable; on the stage we appreciate it since there, in serious plays, we can never escape from separating the fictional character and its creator. Stage burlesque is directed at an artistic method, generally the method employed by an individual player in the treatment of his parts. To caricature Irving was easy; hardly would a cinematic travesty of Arliss succeed. The presentation of this single film proved clearly the difference in approach on the part of cinema and theatre public respectively. These, so generally considered identical, are seen to be controlled by quite distinct psychological elements.

Charlie Chaplin's free fantasy has been referred to above. This, associated with, say, the methods of René Clair, might well serve to demonstrate the true resources of the film; comparison with the erring tendencies of *Once in a Blue Moon* brings out clearly the genuine frontiers of the cinematic sphere. In *The Ghost Goes West* there was much of satire, but this satire was directed at life and not at art and, moreover, was kept well within "realistic" terms. Everything introduced there was possible in the sense that, although we might rationally decide that these events could not actually have taken place, we recognized that, granted the conditions which might make them achievable, they would have assumed just such forms as were cast on the screen. The ghost was thus a "realistic" one, shown now in the guise of a figure solid and opaque and now in that of a transparent wraith, capable of defying the laws of physics. In a precisely similar way is the fantasy of a Chaplin film bound up with reality. We know that the things which Charlie does and the situations in which he appears are impossible but again, given the conditions which would make them possible, these are the shapes, we know, they would assume. Neither René Clair nor Charlie Chaplin steps into the field occupied by the artistic burlesque; neither are "theatrical." The former works in an independent world conceived out of the terms of the actual, and the latter, like George Arliss in a different sphere, stands forth as an individual experiencing a myriad of strange and fantastic adventures.

The individualising process in film appreciation manifestly demands that other standards than those of the stage be applied to the screen-play. In the theatre we are commonly presented with characters relatively simple in their psychological make-up. A sympathetically conceived hero or heroine is devoted in his or her love affairs to one object; at the most some Romeo will abandon a visionary Rosaline for a flesh and blood Juliet. For the cinema, on the other hand, greater complexity may be permitted without loss of sympathy. The heroine in *So Red the Rose* is first shown coquetting with her cousin, suggestion is provided that she has not been averse to the attentions of a young family friend, she sets her cap at a visiting Texan and grieves bitterly on receiving news of his death, and finally she discovers or rediscovers the true love she bears to the cousin. All this is done without any hint that she is a mere flirt; her affections are such as might have been those of an ordinary girl in real life and we easily accept the filmic presentation in this light. On the stage the character could not have been viewed in a similar way; there we should have demanded a much simpler and less emotionally complicated pattern if our sympathies were firmly to be held.

The strange paradox, then, results:—that, although the cinema introduces improbabilities and things beyond nature at which any theatrical director would blench and murmur soft nothings to the air, the filmic material is treated by the audience with far greater respect (in its relation to life) than the material of the stage. Our conceptions of life in Chicago gangsterdom and in distant China

are all colored by films we have seen. What we have witnessed on
the screen becomes the "real" for us. In moments of sanity, maybe,
we confess that of course we do not believe this or that, but, under
the spell again, we credit the truth of these pictures even as, for
all our professed superiority, we credit the truth of newspaper
paragraphs.

TYPE CASTING

This judgment gives argument for Pudovkin's views concerning
the human material to be used in a film—but that argument essentially differs from the method of support which he utilised. His
views may be briefly summarised thus:—types are more desirable
in film work because of the comparative restrictions there upon
make-up; the director alone knows the complete script and therefore there is little opportunity for an individual actor to build up
a part intelligently and by slow gradations; an immediate, vital and
powerful impression, too, is demanded on the actor's first entrance;
since the essential basis of cinematic art is montage of individual
shots and not the histrionic abilities of the players, logic demands
the use of untrained human material, images of which are wrought
into a harmony by the director.

Several of the apparent fallacies in Pudovkin's reasoning have
been discussed above. There is, thus, no valid objection to the employment of trained and gifted actors, provided that these actors
are not permitted to overrule other elements in the cinematic art
and provided the director fully understands their essential position.
That casting by type is desirable in the film seems, however, certain.
Misled by theatrical ways, we may complain that George Arliss is
the same in every screen-play he appears in; but that is exactly
what the cinema demands. On the stage we rejoice, or should rejoice, in a performer's versatility; in the cinema unconsciously we
want to feel that we are witnessing a true reproduction of real
events, and consequently we are not so much interested in discern-
ing a player's skill in diversity of character building. Arliss and
Rothschild and Disraeli and Wellington are one. That the desire

on the part of a producing company to make use of a particular
"star" may easily lead to the deliberate manufacturing of a character to fit that star is true; but, after all, such a process is by no
means unknown to the theatre, now or in the past. Shakespeare and
Molière both wrote to suit their actors, and Sheridan gave short
sentimental scenes to Charles and Maria in *The School for Scandal*
because, according to his own statement, "Smith can't make love—
and nobody would want to make love to Priscilla Hopkins."

To exemplify the truth of these observations no more is demanded
than a comparison of the stage and screen versions of *The Petrified
Forest*. As a theatrical production this play was effective, moving
and essentially harmonised with the conventions applying to its
method of expression; lifeless and uninteresting seemed the filming
of fundamentally the same material. The reasons for this were
many. First was the fact that the film attempted to defy the basic
law which governs the two forms; the theatre rejoices in artistic
limitation in space while the film demands movement and change
in location. We admire Sherwood's skill in confining the whole of
his action to the Black Mesa but we condemn the same confining
process when we turn to see the same events enacted on the screen.
Secondly, since a film can rarely bear to admit anything in the way
of theatricality in its settings, those obviously painted sets of desert
and mountain confused and detracted from our appreciation of the
narrative. A third reason may be sought for in the dialogue given
to the characters. This dialogue, following the lines provided for
the stage play, showed itself as far too rich and cumbersome for
cinematic purposes; not only was there too much of it, but that
which sounded exactly right when delivered on the boards of the
theatre (because essentially in tune with theatrical conventions)
seemed ridiculous, false and absurd when associated with the screen
pictures. Intimately bound up with this, there has to be taken into
account both the nature and the number of the *dramatis personæ*.
Sherwood's stage characters were frankly drawn as types—an old
pioneer, a killer, an unsuccessful littérateur, an ambitious girl, a
veteran, a business-man, a business-man's wife—each one representative of a class or of an ideal. Not for a moment did we believe
that these persons were real, living human beings; they were typi-

cal figures outlining forces in present-day society. This being so, we had no difficulty in keeping them all boldly in our minds even when the whole group of them filled the stage. When transferred to the screen, however, an immediate feeling of dissatisfaction assailed us; these persons who had possessed theatrical reality could have no reality in the film; their vitality was fled; they seemed false, absurd, untrue. Still further, their number became confusing. The group of representative types which dominated the stage proved merely a jumbled mass on the screen, for the screen, although it may make use of massed effects of a kind which would be impossible in the theatre, generally finds its purposes best served by concentration on a very limited number of major figures. The impression of dissatisfaction thus received was increased by the interpretation of these persons. Partly because of the words given to them, all the characters save Duke Mantee seemed to be actors and nothing else. There was exhibited a histrionic skill which might win our admiration but which at the same time was alien to the medium through which it came to us. A Leslie Howard whose stage performance was right and just became an artificial figure when, before the camera, he had to deliver the same lines he had so effectively spoken on the stage. From the lack of individualisation in the characters resulted a feeling of confusion and falsity; because of the employment of conventions suited to one art and not to another vitality, strength and emotional power were lost.

PSYCHOLOGICAL PENETRATION

The full implications of such individualisation of film types must be appreciated, together with the distinct approach made by a cinema audience to the persons seen by them on the screen. Because of these things, allied to its possession of several technical devices, the cinema is given the opportunity of coming into closer accord with recent tendencies in other arts than the stage. Unquestionably, that which separates the literature of today from yesterday's literature is the former's power of penetrating, psychoanalytically, into human thought and feeling. The discovery of the sub-conscious has

opened up an entirely fresh field of investigation into human be-
haviour, so that whereas a Walter Scott spread the action of a novel
over many years and painted merely the outsides of his characters,
their easily appreciated mental reactions and their most obvious
passions, James Joyce has devoted an extraordinarily lengthy novel
to twenty-four hours in the life of one individual. By this means
the art of narrative fiction has been revolutionised and portraiture
of individuals completely altered in its approach.

Already it has been shown that normally the film does not find
restrictions in the scope of its material advantageous; so that the
typical film approaches outwardly the extended breadth of a Scott
novel. In dealing with that material, however, it is given the opportunity of delving more deeply into the human consciousness. By
its subjective method it can display life from the point of view of its
protagonists. Madness on the stage, in spite of Ophelia's pathetic
efforts, has always appeared rather absurd, and Sheridan was perfectly within his rights when he caricatured the convention in his
Tilburina and her address to all the finches of the grove. On the
screen, however, madness may be made arresting, terrifying, awful.
The mania of the lunatic in the German film, *M*, held the attention
precisely because we were enabled to look within his distracted
brain. Seeing for moments the world distorted in eccentric imaginings, we are moved as no objective presentation of a stage Ophelia
can move us.

Regarded in this way, the cinema, a form of expression born of
our own age, is seen to bear a distinct relationship to recent developments within the sphere of general artistic endeavour. While
making no profession to examine this subject, one of the most recent writers on *This Modern Poetry*, Babette Deutsch, has expressed, *obiter dicta*, judgments which illustrate clearly the arguments presented above. "The symbolists," she says, "had telescoped
images to convey the rapid passage of sensations and emotions. The
metaphysicals had played in a like fashion with ideas. Both delighted in paradox. The cinema, and ultimately the radio, made
such telescopy congenial to the modern poet, as the grotesqueness
of his environment made paradox inevitable for him." And again:

The cinema studio creates a looking-glass universe where, without bottles labeled "Drink me" or cakes labeled "Eat me" or keys to impossible gardens, creatures are elongated or telescoped, movements accelerated or slowed up, in a fashion suggesting that the world is made of india-rubber or collapsible tin. The ghost of the future glimmers through the immediate scene, the present dissolves into the past.

Akin to these marvels is the poetry of such a man as Horace Gregory. In his *No Retreat: New York, Cassandra*, "the fluent images, the sudden close-ups, the shifting angle of vision, suggest the technique of the cinema." The method of the film is apparent in such lines as these:

> Give Cerberus a non-employment wage, the dog is hungry.
> This head served in the war, Cassandra, it lost an eye;
> That head spits fire, for it lost its tongue licking the paws
> of lions caged in Wall Street and their claws
> were merciless.
>
> Follow, O follow him, loam-limbed Apollo, crumbling before
> Tiffany's window: he must buy
> himself earrings for he meets his love tonight,
> (Blossoming Juliet
> emptied her love into her true love's lap)
> dies in his arms.

If the cinema has thus influenced the poets, we realise that inherently it becomes a form of art through which may be expressed many of the most characteristic tendencies in present-day creative endeavour. That most of the films so far produced have not made use of the peculiar methods inherent in the cinematic approach need not blind us to the fact that here is an instrument capable of expressing through combined visual and vocal means something of that analytical searching of the spirit which has formed the pursuit of modern poets and novelists. Not, of course, that in this analytic and realistic method are to be enclosed the entire boundaries of the cinema. The film has the power of giving an impression of actuality and it can thrill us by its penetrating truth to life: but it may, if we desire, call into existence the strangest of visionary worlds and make these too seem real. The enchanted forest of *A Midsummer Night's Dream* will always on the stage prove a thing of lath and canvas and paint; an enchanted forest in the film might truly seem haunted by a thousand fears and supernatural imaginings. This imaginary world, indeed, is one that our public has cried for and demanded, and our only regret may be that the producers, lacking vision, have compromised and in compromising have descended to banalities. Taking their sets of characters, they thrust these, willy-nilly, into scenes of ornate splendour, exercising their inventiveness, not to create the truly fanciful but to fashion the exaggeratedly and hyperbolically absurd. Hotels more sumptuous than the Waldorf-Astoria or the Ritz; liners outvying the pretensions of the Normandie; speed that sets Malcolm Campbell to shame; melodies inappropriately rich—these have crowded in on us again and yet again. Many spectators are becoming irritated and bored with scenes of this sort, for mere exaggeration of life's luxuries is not creative artistically.

That the cinema has ample opportunities in this direction has been proved by Max Reinhardt's *A Midsummer Night's Dream,* which, if unsatisfactory as a whole and if in many scenes tentative in its approach, demonstrated what may be done with imaginative forms on the screen. Apart from the opportunity offered by Shakespeare's theme for the presentation of the supernatural fairy world, two things were specially to be noted in this film. The first was that certain passages which, spoken in our vast modern theatres with their sharp separation of audience and actors, become mere pieces of rhetoric devoid of true meaning and significance were invested in the film with an intimacy and directness they lacked on the stage. The power of the cinema to draw us near to an action or to a speaker served here an important function, and we could at will watch a group of players from afar or approach to overhear the secrets of a soliloquy. The second feature of interest lay in the ease with which the cinema can present visual symbols to accompany language. At first, we might be prepared to condemn the film on this ground, declaring that the imaginative appeal of Shakespeare's language would thereby be lost. Again, however, second thoughts convince us that much is to be said in its defence; reference once more must be made to a subject already briefly discussed. Shakespeare's dialogue was written for an audience, not only sympathetic to his particular way of thought and feeling, but gifted with certain faculties which today we have lost. Owing to the universal development of reading, certain faculties possessed by men of earlier ages have vanished from us. In the sixteenth century, men's minds were more acutely perceptive of values in words heard, partly because their language was a growing thing with constantly occurring new forms and strange applications of familiar words, but largely because they had to maintain a constant alertness to spoken speech. Newspapers did not exist then; all men's knowledge of the larger world beyond their immediate ken had to come from hearing words uttered by their companions. As a result, the significance of words was more keenly appreciated and certainly was more concrete than it is today. When Macbeth, in four lines, likened life to a brief candle, to a walking shadow and to a poor player, one may believe that the ordinary spectator in the Globe theatre saw in his mind's eye these three objects referred to. The candle, the shadow and the player became for him mental realities.

The same speech uttered on the stage today can hardly hope for such interpretation. Many in the audience will be lulled mentally insensible to its values by the unaccustomed movement of the lines, and others will grasp its import, not by emotional imaginative understanding, but by a painful, rational process of thought. A modern audience, therefore, listening to earlier verse drama, will normally require a direct stimulus to its visual imagination—a thing entirely unnecessary in former times. Thus, for example, on the bare Elizabethan platform stage the words concerning dawn or sunlight or leafy woods were amply sufficient to conjure up an image of these things; latter-day experiments in the production of these dramas in reconstructed "Shakespearean" theatres, interesting as these may be and refreshing in their novelty, must largely fail to achieve the end, so easily and with such little effort reached among sixteenth century audiences. We need, now, all the appurtenances of a decorated stage to approach, even faintly, the dramatist's purpose. This is the justification for the presentation of Shakespeare's tragedies and comedies not in a reconstructed Globe theatre, but according to the current standards of Broadway or of Shaftesbury Avenue.

The theatre, however, can only do so much. It may visually create the setting, but it cannot create the stimulus necessary for a keener appreciation of the imagic value of Shakespeare's lines. No method of stage representation could achieve that end. On the screen, on the other hand, something at least in this direction may be accomplished. In *A Midsummer Night's Dream* Oberon's appearance behind dark bespangled gauze, even although too much dwelt on and emphasised, gave force to lines commonly read or heard uncomprehendingly—"King of Shadows," he is called; but the phrase means little or nothing to us unless our minds are given such a stimulus as was here provided. Critics have complained that in the film nothing is left to the imagination, but we must remember that in the Shakespearean verse is a quality which, because of changed conditions, we may find difficulty in appreciating. Its strangeness to us demands that an attempt be made to render it more intelligible and directly appealing. Such an attempt, through the means of expression granted to the cinema, may merely be supplying something which will bring us nearer to the conditions of the original spectators for whom Shakespeare wrote.

Normally, however, verse forms will be alien to the film. Verse in itself presupposes a certain remoteness from the terms of ordinary life and the cinema, as we have seen, usually finds its most characteristic expression in the world that immediately surrounds us. The close connection, noted by Babette Deutsch, between cinematic expression and tendencies in present-day poetry will declare itself, not in a utilisation of rhythmic speech but in a psychological penetration rendered manifest through a realistic method.

THE WAY OF THE THEATRE

If these arguments have any validity, then clearly a determined revision is necessary of our attitude towards the stage of today. That the theatre ought not servilely to follow cinematic methods seems unnecessary of proof, even although we may admit that certain devices of the film may profitably be called into service by playwright and director. *She Loves Me Not* with ample justification utilised for the purpose of stage comedy a technique which manifestly was inspired by the technique strictly proper to the cinema, and various experiments in the adapting of the filmic flash-back to theatrical requirements have not been without significance and value. But this way real success does not lie; the stage cannot hope to maintain its position simply by seizing on novelties exploited first in the cinema, and in general we must agree that the cinema can, because of its peculiar opportunities, wield this technique so much more effectively that its application to the stage seems thin, forced and artificial.

This, however, is not the most serious thing. Far more important is the fundamental approach which the theatre during recent years has been making towards its material. When the history of the stage since the beginning of the nineteenth century comes to be written with that impartiality which only the viewpoint of distant time can provide, it will most certainly be deemed that the characteristic development of these hundred odd years is the growth of realism and the attempted substitution of naturalistic illusion in place of a conventional and imaginative illusion. In the course of this development stands forth Ibsen as the outstanding pioneer and master. At the same time, this impartial survey may also decide that within the realistic method lie the seeds of disruption. It may be recognised that, while Ibsen was a genius of profound significance, for the drama Ibsenism proved a curse upon the stage. The whole realistic movement which strove to impose the conditions of real life upon the theatre may have served a salutary purpose for a time, but its vitality was but short-lived and, after the first excitement which attended the witnessing on the stage of things no one had hitherto dreamt of putting there had waned, its force and inspiring power was dissipated. Even if we leave the cinema out of account, we must observe that the realistic theatre in our own days has lost its strength. No doubt, through familiarity and tradition, plays in this style still prove popular and, popular success being the first requirement demanded of dramatic art, we must be careful to avoid wholesale condemnation; *Tobacco Road* and *Dead End* are things worthy of our esteem, definite contributions to the theatre of our day. But the continued appearance and success of naturalistic plays should not confuse the main issue, which is the question whether such naturalistic plays are likely in the immediate future to maintain the stage in that position we should all wish it to occupy. Facing this question fairly, we observe immediately that plays written in these terms are less likely to hold the attention of audiences over a period of years than are others written in a different style; because bound to particular conditions in time and place, they seem inevitably destined to be forgotten, or, if not forgotten, to lose their only valuable connotations. Even the dramas of Ibsen, instinct with a greater imaginative power than many works by his contemporaries and successors, do not possess, after the brief passing of forty years, the same vital significance they held for audiences of the eighties and nineties. If we seek for and desire a theatre which shall possess qualities likely to live over generations, unquestionably we must decide that the naturalistic play, made popular towards the close of the nineteenth century and still remaining in our midst, is not calculated to fulfil our highest wishes.

Of much greater importance, even, is the question of the position this naturalistic play occupies in its relations to the cinema. At the moment it still retains its popularity, but, we may ask, because of cinematic competition, is it not likely to fail gradually in its immediate appeal? The film has such a hold over the world of reality, can achieve expression so vitally in terms of ordinary life, that the realistic play must surely come to seem trivial, false and inconsequential. The truth is, of course, that naturalism on the stage must always be limited and insincere. Thousands have gone to *The Children's Hour* and come away fondly believing that what they have seen is life; they have not realised that here too the familiar stock figures, the type characterisations, of the theatre have been presented before them in modified forms. From this the drama cannot escape; little possibility is there of its delving deeply into the recesses of the individual spirit. That is a realm reserved for cinematic exploitation, and, as the film more and more explores this territory, does it not seem probable that theatre audiences will become weary of watching shows which, although professing to be "lifelike," actually are inexorably bound by the restrictions of the stage? Pursuing this path, the theatre truly seems doomed to inevitable destruction. Whether in its attempt to reproduce reality and give the illusion of actual events or whether in its pretence towards depth and subtlety in character-drawing, the stage is aiming at things alien to its spirit, things which so much more easily may be accomplished in the film that their exploitation on the stage gives only an impression of vain effort.

Is, then, the theatre, as some have opined, truly dying? Must it succumb to the rivalry of the cinema? The answer to that question depends on what the theatre does within the next ten or twenty years. If it pursues naturalism further, unquestionably little hope will remain; but if it recognises to the full the conditions of its own being and utilises those qualities which it, and it alone, possesses, the very thought of rivalry may disappear. Quite clearly, the true hope of the theatre lies in a rediscovery of convention, in a deliberate throwing-over of all thoughts concerning naturalistic illusion and in an embracing of that universalising power which so closely belongs to the dramatic form when rightly exercised. By doing these things, the theatre has achieved greatness and distinction in the past. We admire the playhouses of Periclean Athens and Elizabethan England; in both a basis was found in frank acceptance of the stage spectacle as a thing of pretence, with no attempt made to reproduce the outer forms of everyday life. Conventionalism ruled in both, and consequently out of both could spring a vital expression, with manifestations capable of appealing not merely to the age in which they originated but to future generations also. Precisely because Æschylus and Shakespeare did not try to copy life, because they presented their themes in highly conventional forms, their works have the quality of being independent of time and place. Their characters were more than photographic copies of known originals; their plots took no account of the terms of actuality; and their language soared on poetic wings. To this again must we come if our theatre is to be a vitally arresting force. So long as the stage is bound by the fetters of realism, so long as we judge theatrical characters by reference to individuals with whom we are acquainted, there is no possibility of preparing dialogue which shall rise above the terms of common existence.

From our playwrights, therefore, we must seek for a new foundation. No doubt many journeymen will continue to pen for the day and the hour alone, but of these there have always been legion; what we may desire is that the dramatists of higher effort and broader ideal do not follow the journeyman's way. Boldly must they turn from efforts to delineate in subtle and intimate manner the psychological states of individual men and women, recognising that in the wider sphere the drama has its genuine home. The cheap and ugly simian chatter of familiar conversation must give way to the ringing tones of a poetic utterance, not removed far off from our comprehension, but bearing a manifest relationship to our current speech. To attract men's ears once more to imaginative speech we may take the method of T. S. Eliot, whose violent contrasts in *Murder in the Cathedral* are intended to awaken appreciation and interest, or else the method of Maxwell Anderson, whose *Winterset* aims at building a dramatic poetry out of common expression. What procedure is selected matters little; indeed, if an imaginative theatre does take shape in our years, its strength will largely depend upon its variety of approach. That there is hope that such a theatre truly may come into being is testified by the recent experiments of many poets, by the critical thought which has been devoted to its consummation and by the increasing popular acclaim which has greeted individual efforts. The poetic play may still lag behind the naturalistic or seemingly naturalistic drama in general esteem, but the attention paid in New York to Sean O'Casey's *Within the Gates* and Maxwell Anderson's *Winterset* augurs the beginning of a new appreciation, while in London T. S. Eliot's *Murder in the Cathedral* has awakened an interest of a similar kind. Nor should we forget plays not in verse but aiming at a kindred approach; Robert Sherwood's *The Petrified Forest* and S. N. Behrman's *Rain from Heaven,* familiar and apparently realistic in form, deliberately and frankly aim at doing something more than present figures of individuals; in them the universalising power of the theatre is being utilised no less than in other plays which, by the employment of verse dialogue, deliberately remove the action from the common-places of daily existence.

Established on these terms native to its very existence and consequently far removed from the ways of the film, the theatre need have no fear that its hold over men's minds will diminish and fail. It will maintain a position essentially its own to which other arts may not aspire.

THE WAY OF THE FILM

For the film are reserved things essentially distinct. Possibility of confusion between the two has entered in only because the play-house has not been true to itself. To the cinema is given a sphere, where the subjective and objective approaches are combined, where individualisation takes the place of type characterisation, where reality may faithfully be imitated and where the utterly fantastic equally is granted a home, where Walt Disney's animated flowers and flames exist alongside the figures of men and women who may seem more real than the figures of the stage, where a visual imagery in moving forms may thrill and awaken an age whose ears, while still alert to listen to poetic speech based on or in tune with the common langauge of the day, has forgotten to be moved by the tones of an earlier dramatic verse. Within this field lies the possibility of an artistic expression equally powerful as that of the stage, though essentially distinct from that. The distinction is determined by the audience reactions to the one and to the other. In the theatre the spectators are confronted by characters which, if successfully delineated, always possess a quality which renders them greater than separate individuals. When Clifford Odets declares that by the time he came to write his first play, *Awake and Sing!* he understood clearly that his

> interest was not in the presentation of an individual's problems, but in those of a whole class. In other words, the task was to find a theatrical form with which to express the mass as hero—

he is doing no more than indicate that he has the mind and approach of a dramatist. All the well-known figures created in tragedy
and comedy since the days of Aristophanes and Æschylus have presented in this way the lineaments of universal humanity. If the
theatre stands thus for mankind, the cinema, because of the willing-
ness on the part of spectators to accept as the image of truth the
moving forms cast on the screen, stands for the individual. It is
related to the modern novel in the same respect that the older novel
was related to the stage. Impressionistic and expressionistic settings
may serve for the theatre—even may we occasionally fall back on
plain curtains without completely losing the interest of our audiences; the cinema can take no such road, for, unless in frankly
artificially created films (such as the Walt Disney cartoon), we cling
to our preconceived beliefs and clamour for the three-dimensional,
the exact and the authentic. In a stage play such as *Yellow Jack*
we are prepared to accept a frankly formal background, because we
know that the actors are actors merely; but for the treatment of
similar material in *The Prisoner of Shark's Island* and *The Story
of Pasteur* cinematic authenticity is demanded. At first glance, we
might aver that, because of this, the film had fewer opportunities
for artistic expression than the stage; but further consideration will
demonstrate that the restrictions are amply compensated for by an
added scope. Our illusion in the picture-house is certainly less
"imaginative" than the illusion which attends us in the theatre, but
it has the advantage of giving increased appreciation of things
which are outside nature. Through this the purely visionary becomes almost tangible and the impossible assumes shapes easy of
comprehension and belief. The sense of reality lies as the foundation of the film, yet real time and real space are banished; the world
we move in may be far removed from the world ordinarily about us;
and symbols may find a place alongside common objects of little
or no importance. If we apply the theory of "psychological distance"
to theatre and film we realise the force of each. For any kind of
aesthetic appreciation this distance is always demanded; before we
can hope to feel the artistic qualities of any form we must be able
to set ourselves away from it, to experience the stimulus its contemplation creates and at the same time have no call to put the

reactions to that stimulus into play. This distance obviously may be of varying degrees; sometimes it is reduced, sometimes it provides a vast gulf between the observer and the art object. Furthermore the variation may be of two kinds—variation between one art and another, and variation between forms within the sphere of a single art. Music is further removed from reality than sculpture, but in music there may be an approach towards commonly heard sounds and in sculpture abstract shapes may take the place of familiar forms realistically delineated. Determination of the proper and legitimate approach will come from a consideration of the sense of distance between the observer and the object; the masterpieces in any art will necessarily be based on an adaptation to the particular requirements of their own peculiar medium of expression.

Applying this principle to theatre and cinema, we will recognise that whereas there is a strong sense of reality in audience reactions to the film, yet always there is the fact that the pictures on the screen are two-dimensional images and hence removed a stage from actual contact with the spectators. What may happen if successful three-dimensional projection is introduced we cannot tell; at present we are concerned with a flat screen picture. This gulf between the audience and the events presented to them will permit a much greater use of realism than the stage may legitimately employ. The presence of flesh-and-blood actors in the theatre means that it is comparatively easy to break the illusion proper to the theatre and in doing so to shatter the mood at which any performance ought to aim. This statement may appear to run counter to others made above, but there is no essential contradiction involved. The fact remains that, when living person is set before living person—actor before spectator—a certain deliberate conventionalising is demanded of the former if the aesthetic impression is not to be lost, whereas in the film, in which immediately a measure of distance is imposed between image and spectator, greater approaches to real forms may be permitted, even although these have to exist alongside impossibilities and fantastic symbols far removed from the world around us. This is the paradox of cinematic art.

Herein lies the true filmic realm and to these things the cinema, if it also is to be true to itself, must tend, just as towards the universalising and towards conventionalism must tend the theatre if it is to find a secure place among us. Fortunately the signs of the age are propitious; experiments in poetic drama and production of films utilising at least a few of the significant methods basically associated with cinematic art give us authority for believing that within the next decade each will discover firmer and surer foothold and therefore more arresting control over their material. Both stage and cinema have their particular and peculiar functions; their houses may stand side by side, not in rivalling enmity, but in that friendly rivalry which is one of the compelling forces in the wider realm of artistic achievement.

Realism and the Cinema
by ERIC BENTLEY

Although realism has long been the dominant mode of modern drama, there are two inventions which could—and, according to many authorities, should—put an end to realism in the theater. One is the cinema. The other is the electric lamp.

Just as the abstract painter argues that photography removed the need for representational painting by doing the job much better, so, it is argued, cinematography removes the need for realist theater. Now about the same time as the cinematograph came into use— around 1900—the electric lamp began to replace the gas lamp on the stage. It revolutionized the theatrical medium. It created magical new worlds. At the same time as the stage was outdone by the movies in the representation of objects, it received, by way of compensation, a new power over the non-realistic realm through electricity. Playwrights, accordingly, should—so the argument is clinched—unlearn realism, revive poetic drama, or create new styles for the new settings.

Since it is clear that physical changes in the theater and in society have many times in the past modified and even revolutionized the art of drama, it is fair to give these two recent inventions our best attention. First, the cinema. What effect does it have on the art of drama in general? And does it, in particular, render stage obsolete?

When the nineteenth-century invention of the cinematograph led to the twentieth-century invention of the cinema there arose a new

"Realism and the Cinema" [Editor's title]. From The Playwright as Thinker, by Eric Bentley. Copyright © 1946 and 1967 by Eric Bentley. Reprinted by permission of Harcourt Brace Jovanovich, Inc.

art, not to mention a new business, which in many respects could carry out the aims of certain types of dramatic performance much more fully than the theater. Some felt from the beginning that the motion picture would be the dramatic art of the twentieth century, and this opinion was not hard to support even in the days of the silent screen. Before the talkies were a decade old, even the kind of people who had earlier despised the screen began to see in it the successor to the living actor. In this belief, it is said, Clifford Odets left Broadway for Hollywood: the drama was a thing of the past, the future belonged to the motion picture. A more subtle analysis of the relation of stage and screen was given by Allardyce Nicoll in his interesting and informative book *Film and Theatre.* He tries to find a place for both stage and screen by assigning to each its proper style. The style of the screen is realism, he says, the theater should accordingly be non-realistic. The argument is worth quoting at length:

> If we seek for and desire a theater which shall possess qualities likely to live over generations, unquestionably we must decide that the naturalistic play, made popular towards the close of the nineteenth century and still remaining in our midst, is not calculated to fulfill our highest wishes.
>
> Of much greater importance, even, is the question of the position this naturalistic play occupies in its relations to the cinema. At the moment it still retains its popularity, but, we may ask, because of cinematic competition, is it not likely to fail gradually in its immediate appeal? The film has such a hold over the world of reality, can achieve expression so vitally in terms of ordinary life, that the realistic play must surely come to seem trivial, false, and inconsequential. The truth is, of course, that naturalism on the stage must always be limited and insincere. Thousands have gone to *The Children's Hour* and come away fondly believing that what they have seen is life; they have not realized that here too the familiar stock figures, the type characterizations, of the theater have been presented before them in modified forms. From this the drama cannot escape; little possibility is there of its delving deeply into the recesses of the individual spirit. That is the realm reserved for cinematic exploitation, and, as the film more and more explores this territory, does it not seem likely that theater audiences will become weary of watching shows

which, although professing to be "lifelike," actually are inexorably bound by the restrictions of the stage? Pursuing this path,
the theater truly seems doomed to inevitable destruction. Whether
in its attempt to reproduce reality and give the illusion of actual
events or whether in its pretense toward depth and subtlety in
character-drawing, the stage is aiming at things alien to its spirit,
things which so much more easily may be accomplished in the
film that their exploitation on the stage gives only an impression
of vain effort.

Is, then, the theater, as some have opined, truly dying? Must
it succumb to the rivalry of the cinema? The answer to that question depends on what the theater does within the next ten or
twenty years. If it pursues naturalism further, unquestionably
little hope will remain. . . .

These are weighty sentences, but are they really unquestionable?
One might question whether the drama has always been incapable
of delving into those "recesses of the individual spirit," whether the
movie, even in the best hands, has in fact shown itself any more
capable? But my prime interest is in Mr. Nicoll's remarks about
"naturalism." A generation of movies has given to "naturalism" a
popular success such as no dramatic style has ever had before. *A
Tree Grows in Brooklyn*, movie version, is, one might say, pure
Zola. Mr. Nicoll's strongest point, perhaps, is that the screen gives
the illusion of actuality itself. The screen actor is not thought to
act. He does not act. He is himself and, the argument runs, rightly
so, since the screen must seem to be life itself. Such is the power of
the camera. In support of his argument Mr. Nicoll adduces the fact
that plays fail on the screen, and that movie actors haven't a style
that can be parodied as Henry Irving had. The screen play, more
than any other form of art, is just such a "slice of life" as the natural-
ists had always wished to cut.

This is Mr. Nicoll's argument, but does it all ring true? After all,
we *do* praise acting on the screen; many of the screen's best actors
are also stage stars and they are not always so very different in the
two mediums; they *can* be parodied, and a parody of Charles
Laughton the filmstar is not very different from one of Charles
Laughton the actor; and good plays—witness Shaw's *Pygmalion*—

have been successfully transferred to the screen with little alteration. Nor do audiences believe that what happens on the screen is
really happening or that it has happened—at least no more than
theater audiences do. After all, it was in the theater that the prover-
bial man in the gallery told Othello to leave the lady alone, and it
was on the radio that the announcement of the end of the world was
taken literally. These are abnormal responses. Normally an audience does not give full credence to fiction on the air, the stage, or
the screen. I have known a movie audience to catch its breath at the
sight of wounded soldiers in a newsreel and to be quite unperturbed
by the same sight in a fictional movie.

In short, and Mr. Nicoll to the contrary notwithstanding, I think
there is no radical distinction between stage and screen illusion.
At best the difference is one of degree. The usual Hollywood product does seek to be a convincing illusion of actuality, but so does the
usual Broadway product. This is a matter not of stage or screen, but
of the style chosen by the director or author or producer. On either
stage or screen he may choose, with great effectiveness, to be "naturalistic" or the reverse. It is also a matter of audience. An untrained
audience, an audience of children, might want to save Desdemona's
life in the theater, as at the movies it might believe that it is actually
present in Greta Garbo's bedroom. That is the trouble with being
untrained and childish.

What Mr. Nicoll says is true of current movies and of many audiences, but not of all possible movies and all possible audiences. At
present, it is true, we go to the movies to witness certain illusions
and to share them. We do not go for imaginative experience. Years
ago the Lynds found out how the movie magnates appealed to Mid-
dletown, via the *Saturday Evening Post,* in such advertisements as
this:

Go to a motion picture . . . and let yourself go. Before you know
it you are *living* the story—laughing, loving, hating, struggling,
winning! All the adventure, all the romance, all the excitement
you lack in your daily life are in Pictures. They take you completely out of yourself into a wonderful new world . . . Out of

the cage of everyday existence! If only for an afternoon or an evening—escape!

This is not Zola's naturalism in subject matter and aim, for it is frankly "romantic" and remote from everyday life. It is the naturalism of the movies. It is Mr. Nicoll's naturalism. And it stems not, as Mr. Nicoll thinks, from the medium, but purely from social factors. The movie is an extension of gossip and daydream. It influences life as no art ever has because it influences not as art at all but as suggestion, almost as hypnotism. Clark Gable is found to have no undershirt on, and the underwear trade of America suffers a fifty-percent loss for a year. Ingrid Bergman has her hair cut short, and the women's hairdressers of the nation have to send for more scissors. Not that the theater, on its part, has held aloof from such nonartistic matters. Actors and actresses have often been foci of mass emotion and sometimes leaders of fashion. All that Hollywood has done in this, as in so many other matters, is to systematize what had been haphazard and to make a mania out of a tendency.

The escapist realism of the movies is only that of most popular art. William Dieterle's movie *The Hunchback of Notre Dame* is not different in kind from Sardou's play *Patrie*. What is new is that we have in movies an art form so exclusively given over to Sardoodledom that a man can think Sardoodledom ingrained in the celluloid. Sardoodledom—or escapist realism—always consisted of concealing flattering, sentimental hokum in a setting of the most solid and beefy reality, thus conferring upon hokum the status of the actual and the real. This, it is very true, the film can do even better than David Belasco, because its realism can be at once more varied and more intimate. The camera can find the needle in the haystack and the fly in the ointment, and, above all, the camera—like Mr. Lee Shubert's box office—cannot lie. Aided by the camera, and abetted by popular prejudice in favor of the tangible, a director is able to wrap the maximum of nonsense in the maximum of verisimilitude, a combination as dangerous as the atomic bomb.

We must distinguish between the predilections of Hollywood and the nature of the medium. If the screen is able to be more realistic than the stage, it is also able to be more fantastic. If the Hollywood director is a super-Belasco, the Disney cartoon is a super-Punch-and-Judy, and Eisenstein is a super-Gordon Craig.

Mr. Nicoll makes the movie so completely natural that it is no longer art. He takes the "slice of life" theory too seriously. If we want life, we have it without making works of art at all. We need not pay our fifty cents for it; we necessarily pay in our hearts' blood. The *theory* of Zolaist naturalism has nearly always been astray here, though Zola himself was prepared to define art as "a part of life seen through a temperament" and the last three words are an important proviso. There is art only if the material of life is selected and intelligently arranged. Such arrangement is of course artificial. It imposes form on the formless. And the understanding of art depends upon a prior understanding of this fact. Nothing, therefore, that we take for reality can we also take for art. In a good movie, as in any good work of art, we *are* aware of the "artificial" elements—structure, selection, characterization, cutting—or rather, we can be. In actual fact very few moviegoers are aware of any of these things; but the same is true of novel readers and theatergoers.

A more astute way of arguing that film and theater are utterly different is by pointing to the conditions of production. A movie is manufactured in little bits, the bits forming a jigsaw puzzle which is put together later; on the stage the unity of a single complete performance is the director's chief end in view. This distinction between the two media, like the others we have examined, is not a necessary distinction. It is to equate the present doings of studios with the exigencies of the medium. The degree of decentralization that exists in Hollywood is not a technical necessity. Many Russian directors, for example, have done their own cutting. And, for that matter, joint authorship, in the form of impudent revisions perpetrated by hacks and businessmen, and lack of integration in the directing and producing of plays—these are the bane of Broadway as well as Hollywood.

What then *is* the difference between film and theater? Or should one not rather ask: what are the differences? Let us be content with the reply that the screen has two dimensions and the stage three, that the screen presents photographs and the stage living actors. All subtler differences stem from these. The camera can show us all sorts of things—from close-ups of insects to panoramas of prairies —which the stage cannot even suggest, and it can move from one to another with much more dexterity than any conceivable stage. The stage, on the other hand, can be revealed in the unsurpassable beauty of three-dimensional shapes, and the stage actor establishes between himself and his audience a contact real as electricity. From these basic differences one might elaborate many others. Here I wish only to reiterate that there is no such difference as is suggested by the antithesis of realistic and non-realistic theater. One cannot say, with Mr. Nicoll, that undecorated reality suits the screen, and fine words the stage. Such a belief is a hangover from the days of silent films. On the talking screen the aural is not necessarily subordinate to the visual. One could just as easily argue that the *stage* should stick to the natural, since on the stage the possibilities of fantasy are physically limited, while the screen should go in for poetic fantasy, since it can show anything in this world or the next with its cameras and can reproduce the merest murmurs and the subtlest intonations with its sound apparatus. All such distinctions are arbitrary. The truth is that dramatic art is possible on both stage and screen. On both it could fulfill its function of presenting an account of human experience deeply and truly. On both it would require the services of an artist—I think we may say a dramatist—to plan the whole work as a unity beforehand and of an interpreter or director to see that the unity is faithfully reproduced.

Is the film the dramatic art of the twentieth century then, or is it not? If as yet it is not, could it still grow to be so? My answers to these questions, which we started from, must now be evident. The movies as a whole, like plays as a whole, are a matter of business, not of art at all. The occasional artistic movie, like the occasional artistic play, is one legitimate and welcome form of twentieth-century art. It is not the only one. Moreover, while playwrights have demonstrated for centuries the potentialities of the stage, the screen is as yet an only partly explored territory. We have still to learn what its possibilities are. I have acknowledged that they are different from those of the stage, especially in certain kinds of emphasis. But they may not be as different as many have supposed. And there is no reason to assume that the art of the screen is a threat to the art of the stage, naturalistic or otherwise. Let us question Mr. Nicoll's unquestionable proposition. Although the movie industry can threaten the theater industry, the one *art* cannot be threatened by the other. So long as an art is alive it will be cherished and kept going by the minority that is interested in the arts. "The answer," Mr. Nicoll said, "depends on what the theater does within the next ten or twenty years. If it pursues naturalism further, unquestionably little hope will remain. . . ." About ten years have passed since these words were written. Today one of the few live spots in the drama is the Epic Theater of Bertolt Brecht, which is a new form of realism. That the Epic dramatist believes also in combining the use of stage and screen in the theater is an additional sign that the two media need not part company according to the prescriptions of the doctors.

About Nothing—with Precision
by RICHARD GILMAN

The Sunday *New York Times Magazine*—that repository of everything that has been said better elsewhere—recently carried one of those "debates" about the theatre and the movies which leaves us wondering if our cultural despair is as deep as it should be. Tyrone Guthrie argued for the stage and Carl Foreman for the screen, each man displaying an extraordinary masochistic yearning to make the other look good. Mr. Guthrie said that theatre was more "live," that the movie actor "can't pull out all the stops and stun an audience . . . battering it like a typhoon," and that he personally had never seen a movie that wasn't mere journalism. Mr. Foreman said that films were more visual, that plays were just full of "words, words, words," and that since the movies were so much cheaper you could bring the children.

Any more such interchanges and the end is of course in sight, but penultimately we may find it desirable to choose. As for me, despite the fact that as a drama critic I might have been expected to have lined up behind Guthrie, I found myself rooting for Foreman—or being willing to root for him had he exhibited a grain of sense and had the game been rather different; had it been, that is to say, not a question of which medium was intrinsically better or more important but which was giving us more present satisfaction, more truth and more art. Posed this way, I think the debate can have only one outcome: the movies, whatever they may have been or may become, are currently filling the emptiness left by our theatre's abdication from anything we can recognize as our experience. And only snobbism, professional investments or myopia can prevent us from seeing that.

A handful of movies are filling the space: six, eight, perhaps a dozen in the last few years. Three or four are filling more of it than the rest. As for the bulk of films, someone has said that mass tastes belong more to sociology than aesthetics, a dictum as applicable to Broadway as to Hollywood. Most plays are bad, most movies are bad; it has simply been my observation that almost nothing in the recent theatre has been nearly so good as some of the films of the new Frenchmen, of Bergman, Kurosawa and Fellini, especially of Resnais and Antonioni.

Before going on, I should set down some propositions. The first, which should already be clear, is that the movies are an art, full-fledged, conscious, of legitimate birth and needing no more defenses or rationales. The second is that, while cinema is not so different from theatre as is sometimes thought, what does separate them is important enough for us to be able to locate in it some of the reasons for the movies' present superiority. And the third is that it may be possible to maintain an admiration for the contemporary screen without fatal prejudice to a belief that drama possesses the means to affect us more radically and more durably, whatever its almost complete failure in recent years to affect us at all.

Still, I wouldn't line up any trumpets to proclaim this belief in the theatre's historical and renewable powers. Thirty years ago Antonin Artaud, writing about the kind of theatre he wished to compel into being, said that it "did not intend to leave the task of distributing the Myths of man and modern life entirely to the movies." If we shift to a less apocalyptic plane in order to substitute the word "metaphors" or "recognitions" for myths, we who love the theatre remain in the same position as Artaud, except that we have so little of his at least partially efficacious thunder. The movies are more than ever undertaking our commerce, conducting our transactions, while our desire to get back into the field grows more pious and statutory every day.

I write from the boundless unhappiness and ennui induced by a theatrical season in which I saw more than a hundred plays and spectacles only three of which roused me to a more than temporary acknowledgement of some isolated and hermetic act of skill or passion. There were times when there came over me the raw craving to see a movie: in one mood, *any* movie, as on those Saturday afternoons in childhood; in another, a movie that might be able to put me back in touch with the world, after the deracinations and exiles of our theatre of repetition which cannot find a new tone or gesture in any of its bags.

In any but one, I should have said, and such poor hope as we possess comes from it; it contains the only objects we can dare pit against those beautiful and strange new films that have occupied the strategic angles of our vision. I am growing more and more to dislike "Theatre of the Absurd" to describe the kind of play that breaks, by means of new languages, parody and mockery, innocence, despair and painful fantasy, with everything that is moribund or dead in our theatre—which means nearly everything besides itself. But the term helps isolate what I mean.

"Meta-theatre," "anti-theatre," perhaps "infra-theatre," if we have to have a name. It doesn't matter, except that the "absurd" invites the foolish, asking for Arthur Kopit and Gelber's slipping out of his connection, and that such theatre is only absurd, on the occasions when it is, if you use an old logic to measure it by. In any case, this sort of drama, whatever its future (and I believe the theatre itself has none unless it is somehow along these lines) provided me with the few evenings on which I didn't feel suffocated, when the air was stirring around me so that I didn't have to go to the movies to discover that new and original dramatic shapes are still possible to make.

What is so suffocating about almost all theatre today is its unshakable attachment to and nearly unbroken consecration of what has ceased to exist. The stage throws back at us gestures, inflections, rhythms and grammars that have lost their right to serve as descriptions of ourselves—we are no longer like that, even if the forms persist mechanically. At best, nostalgic reminders of our past; at worst, deadly repetitions of a present we are seeking the means to shake off. Unless we want to note that the theatre also sends us Chayefsky or MacLeish-style mythograms, which are messages from the future, dispatched from areas of aspiration none of us has any intention of ever occupying.

There is a future which we do want art to colonize: the area of our next moves, our forthcoming utterances. The art of the present is always partly predictive, since it tells us what we are about to be. Artaud wrote that the theatre can renew our sense of life by being the arena where "man fearlessly makes himself master of what does not yet exist, and brings it into being." But that is exactly what certain movies are doing instead. When I first followed that long, disconsolate, abandoned search in *L'Avventura,* that arc of despair that led to truth, I knew that it traced what I had been prepared to feel next; that from then on it would be impossible not to see existence with the same narrowed, dry-eyed, precipice-crawling intentness as Antonioni.

La Notte takes us to the same place, by a different route. Here Antonioni leads us into the city, into concrete, walls and reflections in glass, after the rocks, great spaces, sea and terraces of *L'Avventura.* And here the search (or movement; films *move,* are a tracing of movement, and in Antonioni, as in Resnais and the best moments of the others, the movement is everything—events, narrative statement, meaning) comes to the same end, or a fractional distance beyond. The acceptance is made of what we are like; it is impossible not to accept it as this film dies out on its couple shatteringly united in the dust, because everything we are not like, but which we have found no other means of shedding, has been stripped away.

I think this stripped, mercilessly bare quality of Antonioni's films is what is so new and marvelous about them. The island criss-crossed a hundred times with nothing come upon; the conversations that fall into voids; Jeanne Moreau's head and shoulders traveling microscopically along the angle of a building; unfilled distances; a bisected figure gazing from the corner of an immense window; the lawn of the rich man across which people eddy like leaves; Monica Vitti's hand resting on Ferzetti's head in the most delicate of all acceptances; ennui, extremity, anguish, abandoned searches, the event we are looking for never happening—as Godot never comes, Beckett and Antonioni being two who enforce our relinquishments of the answer, the arrival, two who disillusion us.

When Antonioni visited the studio of Mark Rothko he is reported to have told the artist that "your paintings are like my films—about nothing, with precision." An alarming remark, calculated to throw the film theoreticians and the significance mongers into a cold sweat. (Film criticism has always struck me as mostly having the tone of Samuel Goldwyn trying to talk his way in to see Immanuel Kant.) Yet there is no reason to be dismayed. Antonioni's films are indeed about nothing, which is not the same thing as being about nothingness.

L'Avventura and *La Notte* are movies without a traditional subject (we can only think they are "about" the despair of the idle rich or our ill-fated quest for pleasure if we are intent on making old anecdotes out of new essences). They are about nothing we could have known without them, nothing to which we had already attached meanings or surveyed in other ways. They are, without being abstract, about nothing *in particular,* being instead, like most recent paintings, self-contained and absolute, an action and not the description of an action.

They are part of that next step in our feelings which art is continually eliciting and recording. We have been taking that step for a long time, most clearly in painting, but also in music, in certain areas of fiction, in anti-theatre. It might be described as accession through reduction, the coming into truer forms through the cutting away of created encumbrances: all the replicas we have made of ourselves, all the misleading because logical or only psychological narratives, the whole apparatus of reflected wisdom, the clichés, the inherited sensations, the received ideas. In *L'Avventura* the woman says: "Things are not like that . . . everything has become so terribly simple. . . ."

Irony, parody, abstraction, reduction: they are all forms of aggression against the traditional subject, against what art is supposed to deal with. They are, much more than the direct violence which we also use, our most effective means of liberating our experience, releasing those unnamed emotions and perceptions that have been blockaded by everything we have been taught to see and feel. What excites us about these new movies, what causes us to call each other up about them as we no longer do about plays, is the sense they communicate, in one degree or another, of extending the areas of freedom—troubled freedom because a price is paid when you are always half engaged in repudiating your erstwhile captors—that we have gained from the other arts.

I don't think it too much to say that the movies, having come into their maturity, are giving us more, or more useful, freedom than any other form. It may be evanescent, or simply data for more permanent structures to be created by other means, but it is being given to us, a week scarcely passing without some new accession. It ranges from the narrowest and most preliminary liberation such as is bestowed by British movies like *Room at the Top, Saturday Night and Sunday Morning* and *A Taste of Honey,* with their mostly traditional procedures but temperamental and thematic rebelliousness, to the far more solid and revolutionary, because more purely cinematic, achievements of Antonioni.

In between are the films of the Frenchmen, Chabrol, Godard, Truffaut, with their neo-existentialist adventures, proceeding by non-motivation and arbitrary acts, the camera jiggling or running along at eye-level or freezing fast, in not entirely successful visual implementation. And there is Bergman, with his new, not entirely convincing legends, his preachy discontent but also his powerful and clean images and isolations of immortality in a context of abrasive psychology and harsh weather. And Fellini, whose *Dolce Vita* I thought vastly overrated because of its obviousness and mechanical application of its ideas, but some of whose earlier films— *I Vitelloni* and *La Strada*—were full of lucid, plangent vision.

I want only to add, passing over so many others and not even touching on the purely abstract film or the work of the American underground (I am an amateur moviegoer, with no compulsion to study everything and no breviary of the medium), a word about Alain Resnais. He seems to be only just below Antonioni, perhaps not so central, but doing with time what the latter does with space, if the distinction is admissible, since film is preeminently the fuser of time and space. But as metaphors the words might serve.

L'année dernière à Marienbad, Renais has said, is "a mechanism differing from the usual spectacle, a kind of contemplation . . . it is about greater and lesser degrees of reality." And the reality is that of time, of memory and anticipation, the mechanism distributing our ordinary categories, mixing past, present and future, the images from each realm advancing and retreating, fading, reemerging, repeating, coalescing and finally coming to exist simultaneously, the way the mind actually but unavowedly contains them. It is a great film, a "new kind of fiction," as Robbe-Grillet has remarked; when its heroine asks, "What life would you have me live?" we are ready to answer, "This one, because it is truer."

If the movies are providing us with this truer life, this more real fiction, I don't think it has anything to do with the boldness of its themes compared with the theatre's. I think the reason lies, beyond the accidents of genius or circumstance, precisely in the fact that the screen is more abstract than the stage. That is to say, I see the decline of the theatre as rooted in its profound physicality, its being of all the arts (dance is speechless drama) the most nearly incarnate, the most committed to the palpable gesture and the actual word. And it is there, in our gestures, our emotions really, and our speech that we have become most atrophied, most devitalized and false.

What this means for drama is that, being wedded to our bodies and our language, it finds it all but impossible not to drag along with us, imitating our spent movements and utterances. But the film is only the reflection of our movements and statements, and reflections can be *arranged,* selected, reanimated through juxtaposition, interpenetration, *editing.* André Malraux wrote that "the means of reproduction in the cinema is the moving photograph, but its means of expression is the sequence of *planes.*" And planes are outside us, geometries beyond our power to turn into clichés.

When the movies obey their highest nature, turning from being merely another teller of stories to the creation of visual equivalents of our experience, records of our presence among objects and patterns of our occupation of the world, they enjoy a freedom and an authority that the stage has almost lost. Whether it will recover them is not easy to say; there is no magic in our protests that the theatre is perennial, that its loss would be unthinkable, and so forth.

Because our theatre depends so heavily on language, in which so much of our ineffectuality, deceitfulness and untruth is locked, I think it will have to be redeemed mainly by language, despite Artaud's fiery wish that it be redeemed in other ways. And the theatre cannot create a new speech by itself, especially when there is almost nobody willing to listen.

The three plays I saw last season that give me any hope were all works which while not bereft of a reinforcing *mise en scène* were primarily achievements of language, parodic, ironic and outside our formulas. They were Beckett's *Happy Days,* N. F. Simpson's *One-Way Pendulum* and Kenneth Koch's *George Washington Crossing the Delaware,* and none ran for more than a few weeks. I know it is being said that anti-theatre is on the way out. But I can't imagine what will replace it, except something that has learned from it and continues its general action. And I believe we won't have a "total" theatre, the kind of positive, multi-leveled new Elizabethan age certain tiresome critics keep calling for, until we have gone through a great deal more fragmentation, narrowness, indirection and painful jest. Nor will true theatre be anything but a minority enterprise for a very long time.

Meanwhile the movies, with their distance from our skins and breath, their power to make our reflections obey a transforming and arranging will, their eyes less jaded than our own, are beginning to reconstitute our experience. Far-flung, anonymous, their meetings held in shadowy caverns, they are becoming the community of vision that theatre once was. Actuality may be the highest good; when actuality becomes unreal we will settle for true shadows.

Notes on Theater-and-Film
by STANLEY KAUFFMANN

For a number of years I have spent a lot of time going to plays and films, sometimes one of each on the same day, so the two forms are constantly juxtaposed for me. There are some received ideas on the subject of theater-and-film—or theater versus film—that can use a quizzical look. My intent is not hierarchical ranking, which seems to me bone-headed, simply investigation. Here are some notes.

ATTENTION

The art of film lives by controlling attention, we are told, and are told truly except when there is an implication that the theater lives otherwise. The film director controls attention irrevocably; you cannot look at anything in the scene except what he permits you to look at. But the theater director wants to have exactly the same power over you. His job is harder because he has to *earn* your attention. If you look elsewhere than where he wants you to be looking at any given moment, the production is wobbling as badly as when the film in a projector jitters.

The difference between the two arts here is certainly not in intent but in means. Temperament sometimes enables a director to use both sets of means—Bergman and Visconti, for just two instances—sometimes not. Antonioni once told me that he had directed a few

From Performance *I, no. 4 (September–October 1972), pp. 104–9. Copyright © 1972 by* Performance. *Reprinted by permission of* Performance..

plays, and I asked him whether he wanted to do more theater work. "No," he said. "Always the same shot."

The film's ability to vary the shots, to command our shifts of attention with no chance of our demurral, is a happy slavery when the right person is given the orders. But the notion advanced by some film writers that the very idea of holding attention on specific points for specific lengths of time *began* with film is aesthetic and pragmatic nonsense.

TIME

The synoptic powers of film in regard to time are much greater than in the theater. The actor crossing the room on stage has to cross it, step by step; the film actor can come in the door and immediately be on the other side of the room. Film can juggle the present, past, and future effortlessly, and can repeat the moment, *à la* Resnais. The theater can try all these things to some degree (I have even seen the Resnais effect on stage), but it has to breathe hard in the attempt.

Much has been made, quite rightly, of these temporal powers in film. Much has been scanted, almost as if by contrasting obligation, of the temporal powers in the theater. The strength, not the limitation, of the stage is that, in any given scene, time does elapse there, moment by moment. Obviously, figurative time has been used in the theater—mostly between scenes—ever since the first break with Aristotle; still, a strength of the theater is that you feel and see time passing. This is a component of theatrical structure, enrichment, companionship.

It's interesting that in the film form, which can play with time, few works run over two hours. In the theater, which mostly must accept time as it comes, chunk by chunk, many works run over two hours. To see a picture like the recent Russian film of *Uncle Vanya* which, among other barbarisms, chopped the play to bits, is to miss the theater's power of letting lives flow before us in simulated passage, the theater's function as the place where such things can happen effectively.

Also, theatrical time works to the actor's advantage in many cases. A scintillating example was Rosalind Russell's performance in *Auntie Mame*. On stage it was not only a dazzling entertainment but a marathon event. Almost the same performance on screen was less effective because we knew it had been done in bits and pieces over a period of months, and the soft silent hum of wonder as the evening progressed was missing. Almost the only thing wrong for me with Peter Brook's film of *Marat/Sade* was the fact that I knew it had been made in seventeen days—a whirlwind in filmmaking time but a far distance from the span of one theater performance.

"Opening Up"

To continue with a comparison of plays and filmed plays, a relation that is not only commonplace but revealing: The surest sign of the cliché mind in filmmaking is a feeling of obligation to "open up" plays when they become films and a conviction that this process proves superiority, that a play really comes into its own when it is filmed. We can really go to Italy in Zeffirelli's film of *Romeo and Juliet,* so it supersedes placebound theater productions. We can dissolve and cross-fade more easily in the film of *Death of a Salesman,* so the theater is once again just a tryout place for later perfect consummation. We can go outside the house in the film of *Who's Afraid of Virginia Woolf?,* and once again the theater is shown up as cribbed and confined.

The trouble here is a confusion in aesthetic logic, an assumption that we are comparing apples and apples when we are really comparing apples and pears. Fundamentally, the film takes the audience to the event, shifting the audience continually; the theater takes the event to the audience, shifting it never. Just as the beauty of poetry often lies in tensions between free flight and form-as-preserver, so the beauty of drama often lies in tensions between imagination and theatrical exigency, theater form as a means of preservation, of *availability.* To assume that the film's extension of a play's action is automatically an improvement is to change the subject: from the way the theater builds upward, folding one event on another in almost perceptible vertical form, to the film's horizontal progression. The theater works predominantly by building higher and higher in one place. The film, despite the literally vertical progress of the frames, works predominantly in lateral series of places.

The very necessity for the dramatist to arrange to get the right people together at the right time in his one place becomes, for the appropriate talent, a means to beauty rather than a burden. (See any Chekhov or Shaw play.) It is muddled to think that, by "unfolding" these careful arrangements, the film inevitably enlarges the original work. This "unfolding" can be successful when the filmmaker knows clearly what he is doing and treats his film as a new work from a common source, as in the admirable Lester-Wood film of *The Knack*. But most adapters seem to think that any banal set of film gimmicks constitutes a liberation for which the poor cramped play ought to be grateful.

Deep Focus

To oversimplify only somewhat: there are two basically different views of filmmaking—montage and deep focus. Directors nowadays often use both, but we are well aware of the mixture when we see it. In the earliest days of film, when it was discovering itself, montage was prized because it is exclusively cinematic. Griffith, who did not invent it, developed it tremendously; and the great Soviet directors of the twenties used it wonderfully and theorized about it extensively.

This exaltation of montage wavered in the mid-thirties, for two reasons. Technically, the use of sound seemed to inhibit montage; the soundtrack couldn't be snipped to keep up with fast-changing shots. (This difficulty was soon overcome with different approaches to sound.) Culturally, the film became more self-confident, less anxious to prove itself. By the time we get to Renoir, we find a different mode: the held shot, in which the camera may itself move but which is for a relatively long time uncut, into and out of which actors enter and exit, and which has within it different planes. Many critics, including André Bazin, expatiated on this as a new realization in film aesthetics. In fact, however, it was at bottom a realization that the film could use, when appropriate, the 2500-year-old "deep focus" of the theater. The film had come to utilize, along with its dominant horizontal movement, a cinematized adaptation of the vertical.

FRAMING

We often read some version of the following: A difference between stage and screen is that the stage contains all of the place where the event occurs, but the screen frames only part of the film's reality, which continues away from its borders on all sides.

One can see why this idea would grow out of film scenes shot on location. The cowhand who steps before the camera steps out of all Colorado into a tiny portion of it. It is harder to credit this idea when a film actor steps onto a set, even though the camera may eventually go into the next room or outside the house.

The theater audience knows that, literally, what is out of sight is the backstage area. The film audience knows that, literally, what is out of sight—even in Colorado—is a different set of mechanical means: grips, gaffers, reflectors, sound men, and a mechanical omnipresence that the theater never has, the camera.

Seemingly desperate for distinctive aesthetics, desperate, too, to formulate a mystique, the film lays claim here to an imaginative exclusivity that is invalid except to the dull-minded. When Barbara Loden in her film *Wanda* roamed through coal-fields and coal towns, she did not suggest any more real places out of sight than Ruby Dee in Fugard's *Boesman and Lena* telling us of the towns she had tramped through in her lifetime. In both cases there was a literal frame of mechanics and techniques; in both cases there was an imaginative world that stretched endlessly outside the frame.

THINGS AS ACTORS

The difference here is one of degree, not—as is frequently implied —of kind. Vachel Lindsay, with an enthusiasm that was admirable and probably necessary at the time, said of *The Cabinet of Dr. Caligari* in 1922: "It proves in a hundred new ways the resources of the film in making all the inanimate things which, on the spoken stage, cannot act at all, the leading actors in the films." The discovery was important, though overstated. One can forgive "cannot act at all" and "leading actors" in a prophet of 1922; the claim is less forgivable when repeated without modulation fifty years later.

How beautifully Kurosawa, Welles, Ford use *things* in their films —a breeze, a sled, a gun. This is quite outside the competence, or business, of the theater. Although objects acquire metaphoric significance on the stage simply by virtue of having been selected to be there, no one could maintain that they become "actors"—as the splinter in the rain barrel seems to become an actor in *Eclipse*.

But Lindsay's pronunciamento, parroted without qualification, tries to sweep away the affective power of such "things" in the theater as costume and setting. Rex Harrison's cardigan in *My Fair Lady* was a "thing" that functioned for me as well on stage as on screen. Places, which of course are things, can be more easily enlisted in the aid of the whole work on stage. (Excepting the exceptions, like *Caligari* itself.) Inarguably, set design is important in film, and all sets are not equally good. But John Bury's setting for *The Homecoming,* which was a collection of "things," contributed to the drama in a way that was theatrically valid but would have been cinematically obtrusive.

WORDS

Many have noted, myself among them, that words often fight films, which is why classic plays are hard to film. Let's define "classic" in old theatrical terms: The classic style is one in which you must play on the line, not between the lines. In films the action usually stops for the words, the words for the action. In addition, the camera brings classic language too close, as the camera brings the music too close in films of opera. But the facile implication behind this, in much film criticism, is that prolixity doesn't matter in the theater.

In fact, as all theater people know, a superfluous line in the theater is, in its own scale, as impedimental as it would be on film.

Further, when language is designed for film and is understood as contributory dynamics, it is as cinematic as any other film element. Bibi Andersson's account of the sex orgy in *Persona*, many of the dialogues in *My Night at Maud's* and *Claire's Knee*, Gielgud's speeches in *The Charge of the Light Brigade*, Ray Collins' farewell at the railroad station in *The Magnificent Ambersons*, these are only a few of the instances where words, understood and controlled, become film components.

Of course there are still some who think that the film art died the moment Jolson sang. A quite valid case can be made to show that the silent and the sound film are aesthetically separate; but it is a different case from the one that words are intrinsically and inevitably the enemy of the sound film.

The Need for an Audience

We may be coming to the end of the age in which film acting is judged by theater standards. X is not an actor, we are told, even though successful in films, because on stage he could not project beyond the third row; or because cameraman and editor patched together a performance out of his efforts; or because he has to work out of sequence; or because he has the chance to try things a dozen times and to preserve only the best effort. (This last reason would prove that Rubinstein is not a good pianist on records.) Now we are beginning to judge acting by standards appropriate to the particular medium.

Still all performing media have certain standards in common. This can be shown empirically, and it destroys a sentimentality to which the theater clings: that an actor cannot really act unless he has an audience. Think of Mastroianni in *The Organizer*, Huston in *Treasure of the Sierra Madre*, Oscarsson in *Hunger*, Baranovskaia in *Mother*, Garbo in *Camille* . . . and on and on and on. No matter the sequence in which each of those films was shot, can one say

that those are not sustained performances? And can one imagine
how they could possibly have been improved by being done in front
of an audience?

Conversely, there are theater performances that seem to proceed
wonderfully without any real cognizance of or relation to an audience. The three plays of the Grotowski company that I saw were
among the few really momentous theater experiences of my life, but
it is hard to believe that those actors play to and with an audience.
They reveal certain matters; the audience takes them up or not. I
cannot think that *Akropolis* would be played differently if there
were no audience present, or that different audiences affect the performances.

The one element that "live" acting inevitably contains is the possibility of mistake. We are never really aware of the confidence that
an actor earns until he fluffs a line; and it usually takes considerable
time before he gets us back in his grip. The fissure is in a way pleas-
urable because it underscores the fact of the making of the art right
before us and gives us a kind of added pride in the actors who have
not fluffed.

Theater comedy must, of course, take account of laughs, and directors of film comedy have to develop some sense of how to anticipate
what the laughs will be so that they don't smother or rush them.
But laughter is an overt response. Other tensions, sensations, "feels"
are more often than not theater sentimentalities, as far as the actor's
need for them is concerned.

To settle the matter subjectively, which is at last the only way, my
response to film actors is never less than to theater actors just because the former are on film. The medium is never the reason for
response or lack of it. And the fact that film actors *can* move me,
and often do, is sufficient proof to me that they don't need my presence at the time they are acting in order to create.

Most talk by actors about the nourishment they get from the audience affects me much like Don Marquis' Mehitabel reminiscing
about the old theater days, putting her hand on her heart, and saying, "They haven't got it here." The theater has unalterable powers:
it doesn't need to cling to claptrap.

Actor and Role

Any play that we see, we can see again with a different cast; most films never. This is wonderful and terrible, for both the theater and the film.

The London production of *Old Times* did little for me; the New York production did a good deal. Individual actors improve in the same role: Christopher Walken's Caligula, which was good to begin with, was even better when I sampled it again some weeks later. On the other hand, there are numberless plays that have seemed lesser later on because of cast or whole company changes; and the same actor can deteriorate in a part. (Not a rarity.)

In films the performance is fixed, for good or ill. When I urge people, as I do, to see Peter O'Toole in *Brotherly Love* if ever it is revived, I know they will see precisely the same performance I saw. When I urge people to see a play, I hope they will go on a good night.

When I saw *Sugar,* I thanked providence that the performances of Jack Lemmon and Tony Curtis and Marilyn Monroe in *Some Like It Hot* were fixed immutably. When I sat through Welles's *Macbeth* and *Othello* films, I thanked providence that the scripts weren't fixed immutably to those performances.

As has often been noted, most film roles, if they are memorable at all, are inseparable from their performances. The role has no separate conceptual existence, even if the performance is more than a personality display. Who can conceive of an actor other than George C. Scott playing in *The Hospital,* if a re-make were ever conceivable? A film role has no separate existence; most theater roles are apprehensible as entities, even during original productions, because the theater is a place where actor and role meet and, eventually, part. Concepts of actor and role in film may be in as much need of change, *vis-à-vis* the theater, as standards of acting.

Glamour

No contest. Film actors now have it, some of them, theater actors do not. This is a serious loss to the theater, not frivolous baggage.

The mythopoeic quality of actors was an instrument in the mythopoeic functioning of the theater. The theater now gets no such assistance from its casts, no matter whose name is above the title—unless of course it's a film or TV star!

Possibly one of the reasons, among many, for the latter-day theater interest in ensemble work and matrix performance, is the realization that the actor's persona, as armatured by the playwright, is no longer a prime power.

DEATH

No contest. The effects of death belong entirely to the film. Anyone who saw *Wild Strawberries* before Victor Sjöstrom died and saw it again afterward knows that his performance, the whole film, took on added poignancy and truth. Last January I read of Dita Parlo's death shortly before I saw *La Grande Illusion* again; when I saw the film and she came into the barn, I felt suddenly as if more were being given me than I knew how to cope with. It was more than moving, it seemed to confirm the death of the actress herself in a very cruel appropriative way and to confirm, by the very fact that what was on the screen was invulnerable, the certainty of my and my fellow-viewers' deaths.

In the theater, play scripts and photographs are souvenirs of productions, no more, if one happens to have seen the now-dead performers. In film, as TV movies demonstrate every night, inevitabilities laugh at us all.

CRITICISM

The crucial historical difference between theater and film is this: the theater began as a sacred event and eventually included the profane. The film began as a profane event and eventually included the sacred.

No serious person objects to the theater's being judged by sacred standards (as the term is relevant here) because of its origins. But many serious people object to the film's being judged by sacred standards because of its origins.

It is tyrannical and priggish and self-cheating to militate against the profane. But it is a curious critical gift that militates against the sacred, or, more curious, equivocates by insisting that the sacred is *in* the profane.

The theater's struggle is not to forget its past. The film's struggle is not to be afraid of its future. This difference in origins is, at worst, hard luck for the film, not aesthetic or spiritual hierarchy. No Dionysus happened to be available when the film was beginning, but, fundamentally, it was born out of the same needs and to comparable ends. Its extra burden is that it has had to fashion its Dionysus as it goes, fitfully, patchily. But what a proof of its power and its potentiality that it has been able to do it. Why should film be reproved or patronized for this? Why should the one art born in this century be scolded for treating *everything* that anguishes and exalts human beings in this century? Or, more strangely, why should some of its devotees apply critical standards that implicitly urge it to aim low? What a price to pay for being apt!

MAKERS

ACTORS

Acting in Film and Theatre
by JOSEF VON STERNBERG

"THE MANAGER: *Not at all. Your soul, or whatever you like to call it, takes shape here. The actors give body and form to it, voice and gesture. And my actors—let me tell you—have given expression to much better material than this little drama of yours, which may or may not hold up on the stage. But if it does, its merit, believe me, will be due to my actors.*
THE FATHER: *I don't dare contradict you, sir; but it is torture for us who are as we are, with these bodies of ours, to see those faces. . . .*
THE MANAGER: (*Cutting him short and out of patience*) *Good heavens! The make-up will remedy all that, the make-up. . . ."*

PIRANDELLO

The rice fields of Java remain in my eyes as if I had been there yesterday. Standing in the center of these lovely green stretches furrowed with quiet water are the most interesting scarecrows that can be found on earth. High over the rice on bamboo stilts is a palmleaf-covered hut and long strings with hundreds of tiny bells reach from it to the far corners of these plantations. When the birds come for the rice, a graceful Javanese woman lazily stetches out a shining copper-hued arm and frightens the birds away with an eerie tinkle.

The actor is the opposite of a scarecrow—it is his function to attract. The easiest way to attract is to be beautiful. Arnold Schoen-

From Film Culture *I, no. 5–6 (1955), pp. 1–4 and 27–29. Copyright* © *1955 by* Film Culture. *Reprinted by permission of* Film Culture.

berg's wife once said to me with a good measure of unnecessary passion: "How can a person think and not engrave the face with ugly wrinkles?" Though this is far-fetched, it may not be entirely without foundation. It is not particularly necessary to think deeply, but it is, perhaps, superfluous for a handsome person to think deeply. Fortunately, the ability of an actor to think is not subjected to the same strain as his appearance.

The sing-song girl, wheeled in a festively lighted jinricksha through the streets of China, has a simple task. The girls who live on flower boats have a simpler task. They are not required to sing or to move. Not always is entertainment expressed in this primitive form. The rice-powdered geisha in Japan is many steps higher and often has achieved enough grace and intelligence to make her charm and wit the prime essentials. The theatre tries to make use of all these values. Generally speaking, the original attraction of the theatre was carnal rather than intellectual, and is still so today.

But no matter how beautiful men or women may be, they rarely are content to live by looks alone, and the theatre has witnessed interesting combinations of beauty and intelligence. Beauty alone has little lasting effect and so, because of the necessity to interpret elements other than empty beauty, the stage accumulated many who were forced to combine a portion of brain with a portion of beauty.

Though the balance to date is strongly in favor of good looks only, we can observe side by side with it old age and ugliness. This would not be tolerated on the stage without compensating qualities. And we often find those who have grown old with countenances so noble that we know their possessors have worked hard to remove every trace of cheap sentiment. Even when an actor has an apparently repulsive face, his features, on closer inspection, have a baseness of classic quality; and in the ugliest faces are found twinkling eyes determined to present their masks relentlessly to portray the basest instincts for critical inspection.

Trained memories that know the classics, ability to simulate age or youth at a moment's notice, joy and grief projected by precise control of feeling, personal suffering forgotten to portray impersonal happiness; a vast army of actors and actresses lurk in every cultural center to carry out the innermost thoughts of dramatists, to

whom few, if any, human impulses have remained secret. What sort
of human being is this actor and how does he differ from those who
form his audience?

The most essential qualification in an actor must be not to conceal himself but to show himself freely. All those things which move
the engine of our life and which we do our best to conceal are those
the actor must do his best to show. What we are most ashamed to
acknowledge he does his utmost to accent. No corner is dark enough
for us to hide our love, no stage is bright enough for him to display
it. The idea of killing inspires us with horror—it fills the actor
with celestial delight to hold a dagger or pistol in his hand. Death
to us is not pleasant, but no actor I have ever known fails to relish
the idea of showing the agonies of abandoning life, gasp by gasp.
His life begins when the eyes of others are levelled at him, it ends
when he exits from the stage. He is helpless in the face of flattery
and dreams of applause when he shuts his eyes at night. He prefers
being hissed to being ignored, and his private life can be an unpleasant break in his design for living.

These traits have been registered for many centuries, and often
with little affection. Lucian writes in the year 122: "Take away
their mask and tinseled dress, and what is left over is ridiculous!"
Hazlitt in 1817: "It is only when they are themselves that they are
nothing. Made up of mimic laughter and tears, passing from the
extremes of joy or woe at the prompter's call, they wear the livery of
other men's fortunes: their very thoughts are not their own."

A doctor I knew had many contacts with actors and told me that
when he was much younger he had been constantly puzzled by finding symptoms of claustrophobia every time he was called in to
treat an actor.

Claustrophobia is the fear of being confined in a closed room. He
mentioned this to Sigmund Freud. Freud took the doctor by the
shoulders and shook him like a puppy when he was asked why
every actor had this phobia, and roared that everyone with claustrophobia becomes an actor.

It is related that when Sir Henry Irving heard that another actor
was going to play Hamlet he exclaimed: "Good God! How does he

know he won't do himself a grievous physical injury!" I should like to add that the audience, too, can be badly hurt.

Acting is not the memorizing of lines while wearing a disguise, but the clear reconstruction of the thoughts that cause the actions and the lines. This is not easy. In the finest sense of the word, the actor is not only an interpreter, and not only a carrier of ideas that originate in others, but himself can be (though not without difficulty) a good creative artist. He is the mechanic who can take the word of the playwright and the instructions of the director and fuse the two with all the complicated elements of which he himself is composed to give fluent voice to inspiring ideas, with an effect so strong that one is impressed with the meaning of even the simplest word. It is his function at his best to tear emotion and mind apart and put them together again in orderly condition.

The actor also can take the loftiest sentiment and make it ridiculous, and he can take what apparently is an absurd idea and with it illuminate the most obscure problem. He can give us clear sight instead of darkness as readily as a flash of lightning can show what the deepest night contains. He can portray sin for us in its ugliest form and can purge any evil desire by depicting the brutality of the criminal and his tormented history. He offers us breathless excitement and thrill, no less strong because it is vicarious. He can take our thoughts into his body, and return them safe and sound when the curtain falls.

He makes us laugh at human stupidity, and though we prefer not to recognize ourselves, we always notice the resemblance to a neighbor. He can make us howl at the most powerful king, and make us respect a fool.

He can make the ugliest qualities attractive by investing them with charm and grace, and he can take a fine sentiment and deliver it to be absurd.

Those who sometimes stand in the snow and rain to see a tired actor, divested of his trappings and paint, come hurrying out of the stage door, may or may not know that this exhausted animal has just pulled out of himself energy enough to swim the English Channel. But there are some enthusiasts who have sensed that it can be as heroic to struggle with brain and nerves as it is to conquer the elements and have been so responsive that they have carried the actor for miles on their shoulders to his home. They still do that to bull-fighters when the bull-fighter succeeds in making vivid the qualities of skill and courage. But a maddened bull is easy to see. Not so easy to perceive is the problem of the actor.

Life itself may often teach us little except discouragement, pettiness, and care, and we are grateful to those who recall our ideals and inspire courage and give us new and unsuspected strength. The actor can make us walk out of a theatre with determination to conquer our fears, and he can empty our bag of troubles as if we were newly born. The actor can make us aware of the beauty of something we have seen every day and until now thought ugly—he can make us feel as if we have never before really seen a human being, but he can also make us feel as if we never want to see another.

Some of us are partial to the idea that all the world's a stage with exits and entrances, but for the moment, I confine myself to the man or woman who is professionally known as an actor or actress, and who is paid for it, sometimes with bags of gold, though more often with copper pennies. The pay that an actor receives is not a measure of his worth and many a strutter, making as much noise as a sack full of tin cans, has become rich. The acquisition of wealth is a study in itself. Were quality valued according to income the armament profiteer would be the greatest actor. One of the startling tragedies in our profession was caused by paying an actor ten thousand dollars a week and not permitting him to act at all.

I have known many actors and actresses. Some of them were good and some of them were bad, but among the good ones I often found many despicable traits and, among the worst, fine qualities. I don't believe that actors are essentially different from others, nor that they all get on a stage, nor that they all remain actors. I do believe that they seek exposure more than others, and that a lack of self-esteem drives them to solicit praise and applause. The key to this behavior is the same as the key to the behavior of others—it is to be found in the first few helpless years of life.

Since I cannot discuss the great actors who were before my time, my observations must be based on those whom I have myself witnessed. I did see Sarah Bernhardt both on the stage and in films, but only when she was old and crippled, and I have seen all those reputed to be great since. Not always was I impressed. I have been moved and inspired by many lesser known actors and actresses on hundreds of different stages in many corners of the world. But rarely, if ever, have I been inspired or moved by a performer in the films, though I may have been impressed by the film itself.

There is a very important technical reason for this. On the stage an actor is sent out before an audience on his own, though he may be instructed to the hilt. But, once in front of the footlights, he must establish his own contact with the audience and build a continuity of action and thought. The destiny of his performance is in his own hands.

He can gauge the response of the audience clearly—or at least not disregard its testimony easily. He would be a fool to ignore the fact that an intended joke fails to gain response or that an exaggerated gesture is greeted with tittering. (I do not rule out the possibility that fools fail to achieve success.) He is the boss of his own body and of his own mind, knows without any doubt the direction from which he is being watched and himself relays directly everything he thinks and feels to the audience.

All this is not the case in motion pictures. Though the photographed actor is popularized and reproduced so that he can be adored in Bombay, as well as in Milwaukee, and, unlike the actor in the flesh, can appear in both places at the same time, this is accomplished by a mechanism which does not confine itself to multiplication alone. This mechanism not only distributes the actor like popular dolls turned out wholesale, but it actually makes those dolls look as if they could move and speak by themselves. A child, a shark or a horse is made to act the same way as a great actor—easier, as a matter of fact, since they do not resist so much. But whether children, animals, or actors, they are invested with an intelligence that apparently stems from them. In film cartoons, when a tail-wagging duck goes into action, the audience knows at once that behind it there is someone that causes it to move and squawk. When the ventriloquist takes a puppet out of a box, it also is accepted as a unit of intelligence, but the audience is not for a moment deceived about its being a dummy, though it may not care whether it is or not. But when a film actor, who undergoes much more manipulation than a duck or dummy, begins to function, he is judged, praised and condemned, even by our best critics, on the basis of being a self-determining and self-contained human being. This is not so. Actors are usually tricked into a performance not too dissimilar from the process employed by Walt Disney or Edgar Bergen.

In films we have a large assortment of actors with a variety of looks and talent, but they are as powerless to function alone as is the mechanical dummy before he is put on his master's lap and has the strings pulled that move head and jaw. I doubt if many are intensely interested in the mechanism that moves an actual dummy, and it is possible that no one is interested in the strings which move the stars of our day, but I am going to discuss the strings anyway, though they are tangled up badly, pulled by many, and laboriously concealed, after the movements have been made.

Though not wishing to imply that the result may be favorable, it is possible for the actor on the stage to select his material and to appear directly to the audience without any distortion of purpose. But this is impossible in films. Here a complicated machine extracts an essence from the actor, over which the actor has no control. He can be superior to another in proportion to his personal superiority, but his ultimate importance is regulated by manipulators who demand and receive a pliability which, given graciously, results in his advancement, and given reluctantly, causes him to be discarded.

In Paris, the artists lovingly employ a phrase of Cezanne's: "Le bon Dieu est dans le détail." May that be my justification for going into detail, even where detail may be unpopular. The more I ponder on the problems of the artist, the less they resemble the problems of the actor.

Though the actor in the theatre and in films is interchangeable, and can even be active in both mediums at the same time, there are some generally observable distinctions. On the film stage, in contrast to the theatre, the actor rarely knows where the audience is going to be nor usually cares. Often three cameras are aimed at him from three different directions. He can note (to his surprise) a camera leveled at him from ten feet above and a camera looking at him from the ground, both from opposite directions and both recording his movements simultaneously. If he communicates with the camera attendant, he can persuade him to define what parts of his person will be included. He, himself, can never judge whether he is close or if his whole body is seen, since the determining factor is not his distance from the camera, but the focal length of the lens used.

His face is so enlarged that its features may no longer be viewed without discomfort. An inadvertent light can make his nose look like a twisted radish, or it can completely obliterate the expression of his eyes, which usually is a mercy. Though the actor normally is made to look better than he is, the bad use of a lens or the camera placed at a bad angle can produce an effect over which he has no control.

His voice can be garbled beyond recognition by the sound apparatus (unfortunately, it usually is only reproduced) and he can be made voiceless by the dangling microphone swinging in a direction in which he cannot aim his words.

No accumulation of emotion or continuity of thought is easy, if at all possible, to the film actor, as the technique of making a film is such that it sometimes requires the player to enter his house from the street three months after he made the street scene, though afterwards the action on the screen takes place in sequence. The exigency of film production may require the street scene to be taken on the sixth day of October and the scene of the house which we see him enter a second later on the fifth of January the following year. (That shrewd arrangement is called a schedule.) The actor has the most extraordinary difficulty in remembering what sort of necktie he wore three months ago, without adding to his concern exactly what he thought or felt. Notes and drawings on the pattern and color of his necktie help a little.

If he is a genius and gifted with great memory, even then he is at the mercy of the instructions given him by whoever happens to be the most convincing person around. The most convincing person is usually the property-man, the script-girl, his servant, or the boy who measures the distance of his nose from the camera.

I have been asked often why it is necessary to be disconnected in the making of a film. Why cannot a film be taken in continuity so that the distressed actor will know precisely what he is doing? Aside from the fact that there is rarely room enough to put up all the sets at once, or to construct, let us say, a replica of a street to connect with the house which the actor must enter, a film takes from four weeks to an occasional six months to complete. It usually takes an hour and a half to show the finished work. Somewhere in this loss of time you will find the reason for not making a film in continuity. It takes time to build sets, to place the camera and the lights, and to instruct the actors, though this last function is considered wasteful by all but a few directors.

No longer a new medium, the film has absorbed countless men who have attempted to find better ways to good results, and uninterrupted continuity of action has been found too difficult. The actor in motion pictures, as on the stage, is told what to do, but there is no dress rehearsal before an audience, nor a collective tableau to give him any indication that he has been told the right thing. Only the finished product reveals that—and then clearly.

But the finished product is not finished with the actor, but with a pair of scissors. These are flourished afterwards by someone who has little idea (usually none) of what was originally intended and he can remove the most precious word from the mouth of the actor or eliminate his most effective expression. This posthumous operator, known as a cutter, literally cuts the actor's words and face. He can make a stutterer speak rapidly and a person of slow thought think quickly. He can also reverse that process and does not hesitate to do this often. He can change the tempo and the rhythm of the actor's walk and his purpose. He can retain pieces of the performance which the actor fails to consider essential because at that moment he was no longer acting, but thinking of lunch; and with an easy snip of the shears, he can destroy the one expression the actor valued most or the phrase he thought would make him immortal.

He can retain pieces which make hands and legs look like slabs of blubber (physical distortions are less ridiculous than mental ones) and he can cause the most thoughtless women in the world to think by retaining parts of her anatomy that she planned to conceal.

Not only does the cutter cut, but everyone who can possibly contact the film, even including the exhibitor who is to show it, has plans and often the power to alter the film. Actually were each one permitted to exercise his genius for improving a film, nothing would be left but the title, and that is usually debated, too, until the night before the film is shown.

Far from being responsible for his own performance, the actor cannot even be quite certain that the final result will not disclose the use of a double or even a voice which is not his. In any form of physical danger, usually featured in the motion picture, the actor is replaced by someone who is supposed to look like him, and though the actor often is willing to take the physical risks himself (rather than the mental ones), the producer is not so willing since a bodily injury means delay. As for the voice, he may for some reason be unable to sing, or what is more common, be unable to talk.

I have myself replaced the voices of many actors with their own voices from other scenes and in many cases have replaced their voices with the voices of other actors, thereby using the voice of one man and the face of another. Though this is not usual, it can always be done and is to be recommended. (The ideal film will be a synthetic one.)

In *An American Tragedy,* I replaced the voice of the man who played the important part of the judge in the famous trial. This man was not a bad actor, but only too late did I discover that his diction betrayed an accent which was inconsistent with the intended portrayal. I was asked afterwards how I had failed to notice this accent. I confessed my fault but pleaded that the actor had impressed me by not speaking when I met him. Rather than replace the actor himself and hurt his feelings, I replaced his voice, without anyone being the wiser for it, except the actor who must have experienced no mean surprise to see his mouth open and speak with a voice not his. This process is called "dubbing" and is extensively used.

I have corrected faulty diction and exaggerated sibilants by using pen and ink on the sound track that runs with the film; and it has been announced that someone had succeeded in writing on the sound track markings so skillfully resembling the photostatic image of words that, when projected, the human language was heard. Imagine writing the sound of a human language with pen and ink— or changing the human language not only with pen and ink but with the slightest twist of a dial or alteration of speed raising or lowering the pitch of a voice.

Since few are dissatisfied with the voices of our popular actors, little such manipulation is normally indulged in, but ample sections of speech are always eliminated without the actor's participation, and every actor has been asked to make what is known as "wild track," sometimes by telephone. This "wild track" is made to be placed in some section of the actor's performance when his back is turned or when he accidentally waves a hand so that it looks as if he were talking. This "wild" part is usually some tender sentiment that has been omitted by the author or director and which is now recorded separately and then injected into the image of the actor. But normally the voice and body of the same actor is used, though long after he has finished he may be recalled twenty times by twenty different men to patch up something which afterwards passes for a memorable characterization.

Personally, I have frequently been forced to cheat sentiment into the "finished" performance by concealing flaws and revealing meanings with sound and music (all this is done afterwards without knowledge or authority of the actor) and I have had no end of trouble disguising what is technically known as a dry mouth, which means the clicking of the actor's tongue against the roof of his mouth is recorded so that it sounds like the clatter of hail. Such an actor has to be continually lubricated by having large quantities of water funneled into his mouth, which process does not improve a performance.

Intelligent performances have been coaxed out of idiots who have not been able to walk across a room without stumbling, and I have seen intelligent men and women made to appear like half-wits without their being aware of it until they sat in the theatre and beheld the transformation.

Though one can hold the film actor responsible for his person, one cannot hold him responsible for his performance. The more the actor knows about the films, the more he will realize his helplessness and seek to determine the selection of director, cameraman and story, and that process of ultimate demolition known as editing or cutting. But worse than that, until quite recently, not even the most prominent director, except in rare cases (where it could not be prevented) was permitted to cut the film, since the usually anonymous producer had only this opportunity to actively participate as a creative craftsman.

Not many actors have ever achieved the position where they can control the factors which influence their career, and when they have, they rarely, if ever, have been able to avoid failure. The history of motion pictures is littered with the wrecks of players who achieved control of their own productions, though there have been two or three unimportant exceptions.

The average film actor, capable or not, prefers to be called upon to turn on his emotions like water from a tap at nine in the morning—emotions that normally take time to develop—and at the request of even the most incompetent director, the trained star or supporting player will, without too much questioning, laugh hysterically or weep, with or without the aid of tickling or glycerine—and be content in the belief that he is considered to be performing the work of an artist.

It is naturally easier for the actor of little ability to adapt himself than for one with great intelligence, as the system of producing films is more often than not a severe shock to anyone whose mind has made some progress since childhood. But an actor is not easily shocked, and so he goes about the task of learning, as swiftly as he knows, just where he fits into the crossword puzzle of films; how he can function best and how he can sneak past the controls. When he finally is so experienced that he manages to do what he thinks is best without authoritative restraint and guidance, the result is not good.

Not the system alone, but the intricate mechanism and unavoidable complications are against the actor. Usually organized by men who have no sympathy with problems that require thinking, the confusion of the normal studio is ghastly. Everything is ordered except the work of those who actually make a film.

When the film actor enters a set in the morning, the chances are that he has never before seen it (he may even not have heard of the director), but five minutes later he is required to behave in it as though it were a home of twenty years standing and to be familiar with every object. That is not very difficult. He is required to act as though he were alone, but from every possible lurking place electricians and other workers inspect each movement. They are indifferent to his problems and yawn at the slightest provocation, and he must purchase their tolerance with forced good fellowship. He soon is used to that, too.

He may be required to throw his arms around another actor and call him his best friend—without having seen this individual two seconds before playing such a scene. He is induced, and sometimes prefers, to play ardent love scenes to a space near the lens which, in the absence of the leading lady, who is reclining in her dressing room or still emoting in another film, represents her until she can appear. This doesn't bother him at all, for if the woman is present, who for the moment represents the love of his life, she is asked to look beyond him or at his ears, as otherwise the camera, due to the fact that film lovers are not separated by normal distance, makes them both appear to be cross-eyed.

The actor is often not given a manuscript until half an hour before having to act a part (I am told there exist actors who read an entire script and not only their dialogue excerpts) and must take instructions like a soldier to turn and walk to the left or to the right, and be content with the assurance that he is doing nothing wrong and will learn more by and by. If he rehearses too long he is put down as difficult and his reputation suffers. But he never feels that he needs much rehearsal, though he does feel that the other actors need it badly.

With the exception of a very few, whose abnormality should be discussed in detail, I have never known an actor to spend so much time on the inside of his head as on its outside. Apparently, the make-up is really worth taking trouble with, and this phase of his interpretive ability is never neglected. I am considered a martinet because of my insistence that an actor listen to my instructions without dividing his attention with a close study of his curling irons, whiskbrooms, powder-puffs and "fan" magazines. But normally, the director will not insist on being listened to very closely (he may then appear to be delaying the schedule) and his performer lends an ear while the other is belabored by a group whose sole purpose it is to

1. From *Uncle Tom's Cabin,* Eliza crossing the ice. (stage) 1901

2. From *Uncle Tom's Cabin,* Eliza crossing the ice. (film) 1903

3. James O'Neill as *The Count of Monte Cristo*. (stage) 1900

4. James O'Neill as *The Count of Monte Cristo*. (film) 1913

5. Lawrence Olivier and Vivian Leigh, *Caesar and Cleopatra.* (stage) 1951

6. Claude Rains and Vivian Leigh, *Caesar and Cleopatra.* (film) 1945

7. Lee J. Cobb and Mildred Dunnock, *Death of a Salesman*.
(stage) 1949

8. Frederic March, Mildred Dunnock, Kevin McCarthy, and Cameron Mitchell, *Death of a Salesman*. (film) 1951

9. Marlon Brando, Kim Hunter, and Jessica Tandy, *A Streetcar Named Desire*. (stage) 1947

10. Marlon Brando and Vivian Leigh, *A Streetcar Named Desire*. (film) 1951

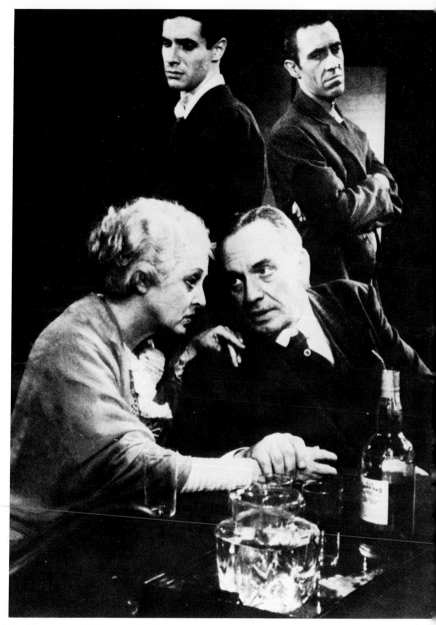

11. Florence Eldridge, Frederic March, Bradford Dillman, and Jason Robards, Jr., *A Long Day's Journey into Night*. (stage) 1956

12. Ralph Richardson and Jason Robards, Jr., *A Long Day's Journey into Night.* (film) 1962

13. Donald Pleasance, Alan Bates, and Robert Shaw, *The Care-taker*. (stage) 1961

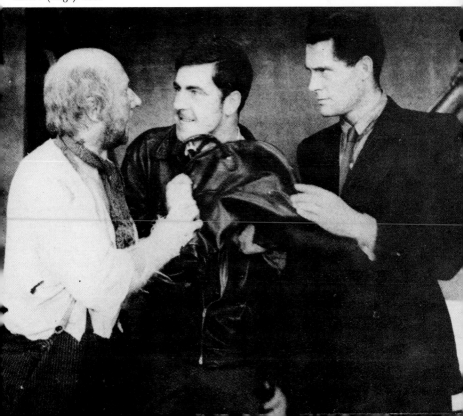

14. Alan Bates and Donald Pleasance, *The Caretaker*. (film) 1963

make his appearance ready for the ordeal of acting. Generally speaking, an electrifying statement like: "Come on, Charles, put this over and we'll knock off for lunch" suffices. Melting make-up is then patched with hasty hands, he is brushed off, hustled and thrust into lights which generate enough heat for a Turkish Bath, and given those aids, he coolly portrays a man of the world while the perspiration runs down his back and puddles at his feet.

If the words he then has to speak in a superior manner prove too much for his memory, he reads them from a blackboard, which is placed out of sight of the camera. These words are usually chalked up by someone whose spelling is on the archaic side. Some of the greatest speeches in film history have been put together from thirty different attempts to read them. Sometimes these speeches have been pieced together from efforts to get the actor to speak them that ran over a period of a month. In showing such a speech afterwards to the thrilled mob it can be noticed that instead of seeing the actor deliver this speech, say the Gettysburg speech, one hears the words while other actors are shown listening with open mouths. Their mouths are not opened because of admiration for the orator's memory.

No, in the film world the actor loves to be known as a man who walks on the stage, views the situation with an eagle eye, establishes quick contact with all and sundry, and then if his name is, let us say, Spencer, to be known as "One Take Spencer." He will value such a nickname more than a gangster who establishes his menace by being lovingly called "Machine Gun Kelly." I once had an actor who said to me while we were rehearsing: "They call me One Take Warner." It took all day to get him to say "Good morning." But to take a scene more than once, though the acting may be execrable, is to waste film, unless the actor fumbles his lines. Believing that every time he opens his mouth the audience will be staggered with delight, the actor is offended if it is intimated that placing words in proper rotation and breathing with relief after every comma is not sufficient to embody them with meaning.

But let me continue to describe this intellectual atmosphere. Peter Arno succeeded in epitomizing the whole absurdity of the usual film stage in a cartoon which shows an actor energetically climbing into

the bed where his leading lady languidly reposes and being introduced to her by the director as he prepares to lie down at her side.
Of course, Arno exaggerates, as the chances are that the actor will
have to introduce himself. With some exceptions, actors do not mind
that. What they do mind is being ignored. There are but few actors
who like to hide. Recently I passed one who was recognized in a
theatre lobby by a tourist who approached him and said: "Aren't
you in the movies? Your face is familiar." The actor turned pale,
mumbled: "My God!" and vanished.

But as a rule, the actor does not vanish quickly enough. Particularly on the screen, where a second often seems to be endless. The
one who insists on staying before the camera the longest is the star-
actor, and one would think that he ought to remember that he did
not become a star that way. But being a star gives him prerogatives.
When he portrays, let us say, an explorer, he will do no more than
don the smeared uniform selected by the wardrobe, and then enter
the stage not as if after an exhausting and dangerous journey, but
as if he had just left his dressing room. The director who points
out the difference will not long remain his friend, I presume. (Directors are usually chosen by their ability to get along with actors, and
with other less essential functionaries.) As for a minor player, who,
for example, is to portray a monarch, nobody bothers much with
him. He is practically booted onto the set by an assistant who, in addition to this doubtful method of inducing the proper kingly mood,
has just shouted, "Hey, Emperor, what the hell is the matter with
you? Didn't I tell you to be here on time?" The same actor will immediately assume the part of a noble ruler distinguished for his wisdom, and issue commands to a benign minister who, yesterday,
played an apoplectic sheriff in a film in which the king was a horse-
thief.

It is also easy to understand that striking story about the man
with a real beard, who was called in hurriedly from the street because the director suddenly had the idea that he wanted a man with
a beard to walk across a scene. The beard demanded to read the
manuscript. The crew on the stage, the actors who were waiting for
this man, the director and his staff, could not credit their ears. Why
should a man who merely had to walk across a stage demand a man-

uscript? The extra, who needed ten dollars very badly, nevertheless insisted, and said that unless he read the manuscript he would not know how to walk or what its purpose was in relation to the story and therefore could no more walk than he was able to fly. It is a tolerably apt commentary on motion pictures that this inquisitive actor was instantly displaced by another beard which did not care how it walked or what for. I later heard that the first man shaved.

But it is not easy to understand why the motion picture actor insists on being rated as a creative artist. He may be a hero or an exceptionally charming individual with fantastic energy. He may be worth everything he gets, which in the long run is usually taken from him. He may be one who chooses this rash way of earning a livelihood rather than another, but creative art has other servants and other standards and is based on no such nonsense.

I was the first to deal with the film machine in *The Last Command,* in which the late Emil Jannings played the part of an extra. If anyone remembers this film of long ago, he might recall that Jannings, who had been Commanding General of the Russian Army, is propelled by fate to Hollywood and there chosen from the ranks of the extras to depict his own history. The picture ended with Jannings driven mad and dying in the belief that he was once more in real command. But this ending was poetic, like all my endings. The film actor is not driven crazy—he is driven to become the idol of millions.

And the length of time in which he retains his popularity does not depend upon him, but upon his stories, current fads—and his directors. The supporting players usually last the longest in their screen life because they do not carry the burden of the failures. They are selected according to types catalogued as fat, thin, monks, doctors, baldheads, beards, soldiers, detectives, diplomats, leg girls, emperors, etc., and heaven help the man who has once played a monk and thinks that on a better day he may be a doctor.

The star is typed as much as the supporting player and strongly identified with the part he plays, not only by public and critic, but by himself (though one hears once in a while that some actor or actress aspires to play something that sounds better than the piffle that made them stars) so that he usually assumes the good or bad

qualities for which he has been noted and is only with difficulty
weaned away from them when another part requires other qualifications. The difference in Jannings' household when he entered it
as a general and when he came home as a film extra was appalling.
He would on one day flick the maids with his whip when asking for
a cigarette and on the next plead with them in a broken voice for
permission to enter.

The nature of his work in film does not allow the actor much
energy for the contemplation of abstract virtue and he therefore
seeks his praise where he finds it in abundance, and he will avoid
any extraneous issues by talking only about himself or about his
part and will not listen to others unless he knows his turn will come.

But there is a reason for this lack of balance in the flustered life of
the film actor. It is induced by the abnormal demands made on him.
He is asked to play a climax first and the scenes leading to it afterwards. He may play an ardent love scene on the first day of the production, and show how he casually met the girl, originally, after he
played the father of her child. These acrobatics are strenuous and
exhausting and drain nerves which are needed to restore normality.

Remarkable is the stretching of emotions which must be interrupted in flow by hours of preparation for each scene, and sometimes by the finish of the day's work which, likely as not, breaks off
in the midst of complications that scream for completion, say: when
an actor is told that someone followed his wife and saw her enter a
hotel with a stranger and register under an assumed name. The sus-
pense will not be broken until nine the next morning.

Failing to be guided by the director, the sole guide to which he
will trust is whether he feels a scene or not. And no worse guide can
be imagined. Acting is not quite so simple. Nor do many directors
care to guide the actor, since they thereby assume a responsibility
they may not wish to carry—nor do I presume that all directors are
capable of guiding the actor.

But then the vital interests of the normal film actor are above acting. Though he will battle to have as many words or close-ups as the
other, he will not inspect the content of the words or the meaning
of the enlargement. He will insist that his dressing room is as good
as the other fellow's and that his lunch when he motors to location

is at least as palatable as the director's, and that when he returns from location that only those ride with him who think him irresistible.

Acting is not make-up nor is it memorizing words. Nor is it feeling a scene. An actor must not only feel but be able to guide his feelings, and his delivery must contain criticism and comment on what he is expressing. He must know when to restrain and when to let go and his intellect must always be in advance of his impulse. He must know why the words that he speaks were written and whether they were given to reveal or to conceal his thoughts. He must be able to listen to the other actor and to consider what he hears, and not merely think of his cue and then act in his turn uncolored by what the other had conveyed. His person may be less visible than the ideas he is expressing, and he must know when his image interferes with or represents these ideas. Most of all he must be in control of the effect he wishes to cause. His humility as a human being must be genuine and not coupled with false modesty because he feels himself to be important. There is no such thing as an important actor or an unimportant one, there is only the actor who gives full expression to the purpose to which he owes his presence. Wherever such a purpose is unclear or shallow, no actor can do anything but be likewise.

We observe how enthusiastic the performance is of someone who dances, skates, sings, rides a horse, or runs to catch a train. But that is only because in those cases the actor knows precisely what he is doing. When portraying a great emotion, the film actor rarely ever can do more than guess where it ultimately will be used—or which of the many attempts to squeeze it from him will finally be shown.

There is another man who may know where all these pieces fit and who is capable of determining what is required of the actor who stands on his stage and who, on occasion with the patience of Job, compels everyone to something which can resemble a work of art. But that is not the actor.

I, therefore, suggest that the motion picture actor can not function as an artist, and will deal with him not as I might deal with the actor who *appears!* to dominate the stage of the theatre, but only as one of the complex materials of our work. Since he has been magnified in importance, you may detect a tendency on my part to incline in the other direction. But my purpose is neither to reduce nor to increase his stature, but simply to study him. In order to do so properly, further analysis is necessary of the personalities who are literally multiplied into three or four hundred images, each of whom can attract a great audience, and can return to the original fame and fortune such as is not gained by a statesman, a poet, a musician, a painter, a scientist, teacher and physician, or anyone else whose approach to his work cannot be reconciled with a failure to master his profession.

The Player:
Actors Talk about Film Acting
by LILLIAN ROSS AND HELEN ROSS

KIM STANLEY

One very famous actor, a leading star in movies who's been very
successful in recent years, could have become the greatest actor of
our time if he hadn't confined himself to making movies. They
were superior movies but not enough for his talent to feed on. He
acted superbly in the movies, but after a while he started imitating
himself. He should have played "Hamlet" on the stage four years
ago, instead of restricting himself to movies. No matter what you
do in a film, it is, after all, bits and pieces for the director, and
that's marvellous for the director but it doesn't allow the actor to
learn to mold a part. In films, it's the director who is the artist. An
actor has much more chance to create on the stage. I'm not an authority on movies. I've been in only one myself, "The Goddess,"
and it was a very bad one. It fell so short of what the real thing
might have been. It more or less exploited itself. And that always
makes a potentially good movie much worse than simply a bad
movie. I don't mean that actors shouldn't make movies or shouldn't
make them in Hollywood, but I do think that Hollywood can't
contain a really great talent, because even the best films are not
enough to nurture that kind of talent. It's in the very nature of

the medium—waiting for lights and technicalities, starting and stopping your part for a take of only a minute or two—that your sustained feeling gets cut off. Good film actors have to be fantastic magicians. A great actor must continue to act on the stage if he wants to keep his talent alive. That isn't to say that any great play is better than any great movie. We need both. All I mean is that when you stay *only* in movies—say, for ten years—your talent feeds on itself. But if you work on a part—even a little part, in a Chekhov play, for example, there is somewhere for you to go because you're the one who is molding your part.

Acting in the theatre requires that you sustain a performance, and I find it harder work than acting in movies. In a film, when all is said and done, good cutting can make a good actor out of a donkey. I never go to see myself in the movies—thanks to Bernard Shaw, really. I once said to him that it might be a good idea to go and see yourself, as a way of seeing what you do and learning to correct your faults. You're more likely, he told me, to destroy your virtues. If you watch yourself in the movies, you become terribly self-conscious and begin trying to make yourself like other people, when the one thing you have that counts as an actor is whatever you have that makes you different. You don't ever want to destroy that individuality. Theatre acting gives you a rehearsal period of three weeks. The movies don't allow time. During rehearsals for the stage, you adapt the character to yourself just as much as you adapt yourself to the character. You begin to feel it's right when you feel one little bit of it is right. The rest of it will then fall into place. You have an awareness of what you're doing, but it's instinctive.

MELVYN DOUGLAS

In 1931, I went out to Hollywood under contract to Samuel Goldwyn, at a salary of nine hundred dollars a week. My first movie was the filmed version of "Tonight or Never," with Gloria Swanson playing the lead. She was at the height of her career, and the rumor was that she was going to make four pictures a year, at two hundred and fifty thousand dollars a picture. She'd arrive on the set with a retinue of servants, and at four o'clock she'd stop work. The servants would serve tea from a silver service, and we'd sit around and chat. Then we'd wrap up and go home. With that kind of beginning, I got an erroneous impression of how movies were made. Not many were made like that even in those halcyon days. I found the mechanics fascinating and exciting, and utterly different from anything I had known in the theatre. At first, I was impressed by the tricks—the miniatures used for sets, the staging of crowd scenes. Then I became aware of the difference in the acting. It seemed to me that acting in movies was personality exploitation. Acting was the most important part to me, and I found out after a while that it wasn't very interesting. I didn't think I was very good in movies. I didn't think I was photogenic. I didn't feel I belonged. I thought I was a run-of-the-mill leading man. I didn't like it. I was a body slave to the producers, like a ballplayer. I had neither the time nor the ability to enjoy what I was doing.

My second movie, "As You Desire Me," based on Pirandello's play, was with Greta Garbo. It was the first of three movies I made with her. She was a provocative girl. I found working with her an extraordinary experience. She wasn't a trained actress—and she was aware of that herself—but she had extraordinary intuitions, especially in the realm of erotic experience. I've never seen anything like her sensitive grasp of colors and shadings. Her acting made you feel that here was a woman who knew all there was to know about all aspects of love. I think her "Camille" is one of the greatest things of all time as a fantastic portrait of a woman in love. I was a little awestruck by Garbo at first, but I found her a very easy person to be with. We talked about everything, including her awareness of how she'd never really learned to be an actress. She was much more adept in the love scenes than in any other scenes. This impression was reinforced in my two other pictures with her—"Ninotchka" and "Two-Faced Woman." She produced an extraordinarily comic effect in "Ninotchka," not so much because of any comic sense she may have had as through the genius of the director, Ernst Lubitsch; he knew just how to make use of the stolid Scandinavian in her. But her love scenes left all of us astonished. She was utterly superb. In the scene in "Ninotchka" in which we come back to the hotel after drinking champagne and she behaves like a girl in love, she achieved a quality and a feeling that were literally breathtaking.

Movies give you a kind of buildup and national reputation that aren't always possible in the theatre. Altogether, I made fifty or sixty movies. Occasionally, now, I watch myself in them on television, and my feelings about what I see range from horror to some slight pleasure. I'm interested and amused to see what I did in those movies. By 1942, I was earning thirty-five hundred dollars a week, with a guarantee of at least forty weeks' work a year. I'd make over a hundred and eighty thousand dollars a year. But the money very soon ceased to be an attraction for me. Almost every part I played was a series of ghastly frustrations, especially when I had the kind of director I couldn't hold an intelligible conversation with, and I had a lot of that kind. If you work with an open-minded director, the part can become a voyage of exploration and discovery. Otherwise, it's just a matter of "Does the uniform fit properly?" and "Does he know his lines?" and "Let's shoot it." I rarely carried away the feeling of having lived through the experience of my part; I carried away only the memory of the plot and some of my own lines. Of all the movies I made, I liked just two or three, and that was chiefly because of the directors. The pleasure and satisfaction came from my relationship with the directors, rather than from the parts I played. Under the direction of Ernst Lubitsch, I had great pleasure making "Angel," with Marlene Dietrich and Herbert Marshall, and "That Uncertain Feeling," with Merle Oberon and Burgess Meredith. It was always a joy to work with Lubitsch. To begin with, he was an enormously engaging man, and brilliantly imaginative. Attempted imitations of his work are still going on in Hollywood, but the imitations don't come off. It's like trying to imitate a writer by using some of the same words he uses. Lubitsch loved actors. He loved seeing an actor's wit work. If the actor had anything to offer, Lubitsch had the ability to stimulate his imaginative processes, to help him find nuances of character and amusing ways of doing things. And you felt you could rely on his taste, which is a wonderful thing for an actor to be able to feel. One other man I was grateful to and happy to work with was Richard Boleslawski, who directed me in "Theodora Goes Wild," with Irene Dunne. He was a really creative guy, too—different from Lubitsch, but another one of the kind you always hope to find working in a supposedly creative field. Boleslawski was a person of substance, of taste and imagination, who was completely articulate and was able to make his own quality felt in his movies.

After nine or ten months in Hollywood, under contract to Goldwyn, I got so I hated it. My wife didn't make movies; while I worked in pictures, she worked in the theatre in Los Angeles. I had a seven-year contract, but in 1932 I was able to get out of it, and my wife and I took a trip around the world. We returned from Japan to California, where our son Peter was born. In January, 1934, I went back into the legitimate theatre, playing the lead in "No More Ladies," by A. E. Thomas. My wife went to Hollywood during that season to do "She," the only picture she ever made, and when my play closed, I went out there to spend the summer with her. While I was hanging around, I was put under a joint contract by Columbia Pictures and M-G-M. Columbia asked me to do a film called "She Married Her Boss," with Claudette Colbert. I agreed. They made it a condition that I do three pictures a year for seven years, with options. I did that, never thinking they'd pick my option up. But that first movie turned out to be one of the most successful pictures Columbia ever made, and the studio did pick up the option. So there I was, stuck again, and feeling that I was in the wrong place again—that it was the theatre that was natural to me. Then they began to give me the same kind of part over and over. My comedy role in that one successful movie was a salable commodity; they began exploiting what was supposed to be the comic Melvyn Douglas. Think of what M-G-M did to a fine actor like Frank Morgan. He just happened to do a few trick laughs in a picture, and from then on that was *all* that Frank Morgan did. I earned what became an international reputation for being one of the most debonair and witty farceurs in Hollywood. I was cut off from the world I knew.

HENRY FONDA

It was easy to make the transition to movies. I started to act in the film version of "The Farmer Takes a Wife" the way I always did for a play, and Victor Fleming, the director, told me I was mugging. And that's all it took. I just pulled it down to reality. You don't project anything for movies. You do it as you would in your own home. Because of all the experience back of me in the same part, it didn't bother me to work out of continuity, the way you do in making a movie. Of course, there's very little personal satisfaction in doing those bits and pieces for a movie. You don't really have any recollection of having created a role. But in the beginning the money made it pretty attractive. After doing "The Farmer Takes a Wife," I made two movies for Wanger—"The Trail of the Lonesome Pine," with Sylvia Sidney, and "The Moon's Our Home," with Margaret Sullavan. I wanted to get my feet back on the boards, but I wasn't getting any plays submitted to me, and I kept making more movies, including "Jezebel," with Bette Davis, "Jesse James," with Tyrone Power, and "Young Mr. Lincoln," in which I played the title role. One movie I was eager to do was "The Grapes of Wrath"—the part of Tom Joad—and I had to sign a seven-year contract with Fox to get the part. I regretted it, but signed. Then I couldn't get out of the contract. I made all kinds of movies I hated. My gorge rises when I remember them. I did make a few I liked, though, including "The Lady Eve" and "The Male Animal," on loan-out. After "The Grapes of Wrath," I made "The Ox-Bow Incident," but it took long sessions of violent argument with Darryl Zanuck to get him to allow me to do it. In 1956, I acted in "12 Angry Men," which I co-produced with Reginald Rose, and which won many awards. I'm prouder of that than of almost anything else I've done in my career. . . .

The theatre is where I really get my kicks. When you make a movie, and people say you're great, you like to hear them say it, but you don't have the feeling you've lived your character or built your emotions one on top of another. In movies, you hit emotion maybe once in a scene. Live television is like the theatre. You're on and you're committed to it, the way you are on the stage. Film television is like movies. You do television movies to make a buck and save a buck. I was damn lucky I became an actor. Theatre is the only thing I understand. I can't really talk about anything else. In company, I don't have small talk. It's pretty silly to begin with, and I don't know how to do it at all. When you've exhausted the weather, and where you've been, and where they've been, you're stuck. When I get stuck, I feel everybody is looking at me and I want to hide. I like to be the observer.

FRANÇOISE ROSAY

In the theatre, I like all the work onstage, and I also like the rehearsals. But I do not like the effect that the audience has on the acting. You wait for them to laugh, you wait for them to cry, instead of concentrating all your attention on the acting itself. It is like being a painter and waiting for the people to come and tell you they like this color or that, dislike this one or that. And, *en passant,* I will say that I do not like to bow. Altogether, acting in films is much better. You do not wait for the public to react. And the day after you do a scene you can study the film and see what you did wrong, so that you can correct your errors as you go along. Whereas on the stage you do a whole performance and then there you are—it is gone, beyond repair.

Whether for the stage or the films, acting ability is a gift. It has nothing to do with intelligence. I have known one or two great actors who were perfectly stupid and yet looked very intelligent on the stage. For the stage, of course, an actor has to have the vocal power and has to articulate; he has to make himself heard and understood. But for any kind of acting you have to observe a lot, and read a lot.

ROD STEIGER

I enjoy working in television and in movies as much as I do in the theatre. Each medium has its drawbacks. Live television is the most difficult to do, because you have all the pressure of an opening night in the theatre, and no chance to correct or change what you do. An actor can develop tremendously in live television if he has some background and training. I used to do two or three shows a month, with only five days of rehearsal for a half-hour drama. It was wonderful training and discipline. Unfortunately, live television plays have become a thing of the past. Big money got into television in 1954 and flattened it. But live television is still the closest thing to a repertory theatre, which is the best kind of training in the development of an actor. The essence of playing in a movie is remembering that it's always the picture that is important, not the words. In the theatre, as in live television, you must have the training to sustain your performance. In movies, you can get away with a lot, because you don't have to sustain your performance for more than two or three minutes at a time. If you're only a personality, without talent, and you're photographed right, you can look like an actor in the movies, but the beauty of humanness is always sacrificed for surface appearances. In New York, you're in competition with other actors. In Hollywood, there is always the possibility that you may have to compete with anybody who can be photographed effectively. Wherever an actor is and whatever he's doing, he must maintain his discipline. When your mind is alert, your performance is alert. When you're disturbed or tired, your performance suffers. That's why I'll never stay in a play for longer than six months. There's too much chance that you may start to play it automatically.

DANA ANDREWS

Every person, whether he's an actor or not, has his own way of communicating with other people. If your personality is unusual

enough, you can become a star in the movies. You can't get rid of
your own personality. It's going to come through, no matter what
you're doing. In certain ways, it's harder to act in the movies than
on the stage. The camera is so close. It sees so much and shows
so much. It picks up every little thing you do with your eyes and
mouth. On the stage, you don't have to be so conscious of every
little gesture. On the stage, you can lose yourself in the role more
and let what happens just happen. You get a much better opportunity on the stage to develop the character you're playing. Working
in the continuity of a play—rather than in snatches, out of continuity, in a movie—gives you a better view of the work as a whole,
and a deeper understanding of it. Having an audience right there
while you're acting is immensely satisfying. The handicaps you
have in stage acting that you don't have in movies are minimal—
projecting to the rear of the theatre, remembering lines, playing so
that everything is visible and audible to the audience. I replaced
Henry Fonda in "Two for the Seesaw" on Broadway for a year, and
it was an experience I shall never forget. I didn't miss a single performance—not even one time when I had a temperature of a hundred and three. You can grow on the stage. After a year of playing
the lead, I had just begun to understand it, to understand what
the author meant me to be. When I started out in the play, I was
overemotional. Because I was playing the part of a self-pitying man,
I had a tendency to whine. My wife pointed that out to me, and I
found that if a man feels sorry for himself, he doesn't have to whine
to show it. I stopped whining at once. It's not difficult for me to
hide emotion, since I've always hidden it in my personal life. What
is difficult is to convey feelings in a quiet and reserved way. Coming to Broadway after twenty years in Hollywood appealed to me.
When I came to Broadway, I was looking for a kind of revitaliza-
tion. I found it. Playing on the stage demands total concentration,
and absolute devotion to the part you're playing. I'm unaware of
the audience except when it isn't with me. When the throat-clear-
ing, coughing, and squirming start, I know I have to put in a little
more effort. I need to get the people back with me. Then I can
forget them. In movies, I had been a leading man, and in movies
a leading man is usually a man who can do no wrong. I was ex-

pected to play pleasantly, to play pleasingly, to play a good man who is always victorious over evil. I've always thought of it as being a boom-boom-boom actor. I'd outshout, outfight, outcharm, out-everything everybody while acting. Meanwhile, the real acting parts were going to the character actors. After all those years in movies, my senses as an actor were dulled. On the stage, it was up to me to hold the interest of the people out there in the audience. I wasn't expected to boom-boom-boom away. I was expected to *act*. That one thing made all the difference. Everything was before me, and the possibilities were endless.

RICHARD WIDMARK

From the beginning, what I always had in mind was eventually to go to Hollywood. I wanted to act in movies more than in plays. . . .

My first movie, and my part in it as a laughing murderer who pushes an old lady down some stairs and kills her, practically gave me a phobia. I'd never seen myself on the screen, and when I did I wanted to shoot myself. That damn laugh of mine! For two years after that picture, you couldn't get me to smile. I played the part the way I did because the script struck me as funny and the part I played made me laugh, the guy was such a ridiculous beast. I was doing "Inner Sanctum" on radio at the same time, and I remember reading the "Kiss of Death" script to some of the guys and saying "Hey, get a load of this!" and laughing, it was so funny. And that's the way I played the part in the movie. Movie audiences fasten on to one aspect of the actor; they hold on to a piece of your personality for dear life, and decide what they want you to be. They think you're playing yourself. The truth is that the only person who can ever really play himself is a baby. You seldom learn to act in movies. I learned the fundamentals on the stage. In movies, you learn to do things on a minute scale, and there's nowhere to go from there. If you start in the theatre, you can learn later how to scale things down for pictures. Movie acting, however, is the most difficult kind of all to do. Theatre acting is a breeze by comparison.

The fact that you're working on comparatively short fragments in a movie, out of context, and that you have to make them all add up to a whole is difficult enough. But then you have all the mechanical paraphernalia around. True movie acting is such a rare thing.

MICHAEL REDGRAVE

I didn't take to movie-making at first, though I love it now. At the time, I signed for pictures reluctantly, with Gainsborough Pictures. The pay was tempting. Nobody prepared me in the beginning for the horrors of picture-making. Nobody explained it to me. I think I got the contract by doing a test for which I didn't give a damn. I was playing with this wonderful galaxy at night and let everyone know it during the day. Naturally, Alfred Hitchcock, the director of the picture—it was "The Lady Vanishes"—did everything to take me down a peg. My second picture, "Stolen Life," was with Elisabeth Bergner, a great actress and one I adored, and although the picture was not very good, I enjoyed making it. The director, Paul Czinner, told me that films could do something special that stage acting could not; there was a spontaneity that the camera could catch when you were first feeling your way in a part, before it became too polished. On the stage, one would work for weeks to achieve a certain thing, but the movie camera could catch something early that was more effective on the screen than the polished thing. One of the movies I enjoyed doing most was "Dead of Night." I also enjoyed "The Browning Version" and "The Dam Busters," and there have been a number of others that have caught my imagination. But I confess that many of the pictures I have made I have accepted because the money they brought me helped me to choose in the theatre only the parts I liked. "Dead of Night" is the one of the films that many people, oddly enough, seem to remember me for. I played the role of a mad ventriloquist. The director of my sequence in the film was Alberto Cavalcanti, and something happened, the kind of thing that happens when a particular actor meets a particular director who excites his invention in a particular part and works with him on a give-and-take basis. Perhaps it's too easy an answer, but I've always believed to a certain degree that the effectiveness of a film part depends on whether you can say in one sentence, or on a postcard, what the part is. For example, about my part in "Dead of Night" you can say, "It's about a ventriloquist who believes his life is controlled by his dummy." And everyone then is able to say "Ah!" I don't think you can describe Hamlet on a postcard. A film has a more immediate impact than a stage play, which is not necessarily an advantage for the actor. Hamlet leaves a deeper impression on you when played on the stage than any role I can think of in a film. There are differences in the satis-faction I get in acting in the two mediums. Some of the most ex-citing moments in the theatre come in rehearsals, when you're first discovering or exploring a part. The camera can catch these early moments on film. But in the theatre you go on for several weeks making natural each time what would otherwise become stale. Dur-ing rehearsals, you find the little truths, and as time goes on, you can work to enlarge your part without making it seem enlarged. I made two films in Hollywood in 1947—"Mourning Becomes Electra," which didn't come off as a story told through a lens and "Secret Beyond the Door," directed by Fritz Lang. Hollywood was all right for three months, but when I stayed on to make the second picture, I couldn't take the publicity, the status symbols, and all that foolishness.

ANGELA LANSBURY

I like acting in movies better than on the stage, because you don't have to keep on and on with it. I'm a traitor to the cause. I don't indulge myself in the enjoyment of acting. I have a tremendous sense of duty about the theatre. For instance, I have a strong sense of guilt about being late. I become all professional as soon as I leave my home—as soon as I have my coat on and am on my way. I feel I have to be early. And if I don't put the makeup on just right, I worry about it all night. I have a great sense of responsibility. Maybe that's the reason I can't enjoy it.

ANTHONY QUINN

In the theatre, you play to the audience. In moviemaking, the director is your audience, and if he's pleased, you feel you've done your job. In the theatre, you've got a whole new crowd out there every night. You can become mesmerized by the feeling of acceptance you get from them. You have to keep yourself in check. Sometimes you have to step on a laugh, if you know it's a bad laugh you're getting. Only the amateur actor looks to make himself feel good. The pro takes his work seriously and has a constant awareness of the battle to tell the truth. A bad actor feels good after a performance, but the pro feels only the responsibility for finding the truth, no matter what. Some actors say "How much of me is like this part?" and others say "How much of me is *not* like this part?" I always try to see myself in the part. You create your own propulsion for going onstage each night. Olivier is a dedicated actor. His standards are extremely high. He is a model of discipline. But I have to work differently from the way he works. He finds the truth offstage and brings it with him; I try to find the truth onstage. I'm searching for it; he's already got it. The closest thing to acting is bullfighting or boxing. It's a matter of adjusting to the other man's blows. You're so busy adjusting it's difficult to think of anything else. Your images control your movements. It's a way of life—the same all over the world. The actor is an artist. He comments on life constantly. He's a true creator. No one has more latitude to create than an actor. I can conjure up all the images I want, with perfect freedom, and what are the words until I say them? Before I go onstage, I experience the tremendous thrill of knowing that I will feel love, hate, anger, and will transmit them to the audience. My objective is now clear. What I want to do is to create, to say what I have to say.

JASON ROBARDS, SR.

In 1950, after doing a play again on Broadway, I didn't like the idea of going back to work in Hollywood television movies of the conveyor-belt kind, but sometimes you have to go back to all those "Cimarron City"'s in order to live. I'll never forget what Jason said to me when I was going to be in that play with him. "This isn't any father-son deal," he said. "We're two actors together, and we won't give an inch." Real life for an actor is in the living theatre. There is *nothing* that compares with the living theatre. It's like telling a story and having someone to *listen* to you. If there's no one in the room who cares what you say, if your only audience is the cold camera eye, if you bobble a line or slur a word and there's a mechanic to yell "Cut!" and you do it over again, you feel more and more that something important is being taken away from you. In the living theatre, you have the challenge right there with you —this is it, hot or cold, for better or worse, this is *it*. The audience out there cares—cares what you're doing, cares to hear what you're saying, cares to respond to what is happening on the stage. Why, in movies I've walked in at the start of a picture and not even known the people I was playing with. The important things were the lights, the dollies, the cold camera eye. The other actors had never seen me before, and I had never seen them. We'd have that little embarrassed thing where we all said our names. Then we'd have a run-through. Then the camera would shoot it. In less than a day, you pick up your script, put on your makeup, get your wardrobe, and meet your fellow-actors, and then the machine gets to work on you. In the old days of quickies, I'd make a full-length feature picture in one week. How does that compare with being in the *theatre?* With four or five weeks of careful rehearsing, people looking into each other's eyes—real, living people? You're in a state of well-being. You can't find it in any other way. Everything else is blotted out. It's plain joy. It keeps you alive. Jason's elder boy, Jason III, is twelve and likes acting, too, and has already been in grammar-school plays in New York. Jason and I talk about getting up a play for the three of us to be in together.

ANTHONY PERKINS

Of the various kinds of acting, I prefer the stage. I played the part of Eugene Gant in "Look Homeward, Angel," by Ketti Frings,

and the part of Gideon, the young man, in the Frank Loesser musical "Greenwillow." After Hollywood, being on the stage felt great.
You can't separate the actor from the circumstances in which he
works. When you act in a picture, the director can threaten and
bully you or else let you do it your own way and then just cut it
out of the picture and not show it at all. The only way to keep
control over what you do is to act on the stage. Once you walk out
there, nobody can shout at you or pull strings and get you to jump.
Once you're out there acting, you're doing it on your own. Life in
Hollywood is corrosive for the actor. The minute you're through
making a picture, you're an actor out of a job. It's over. If you're
a big star, theoretically you have no worries, but even if you're the
kingpin, all you can do is play croquet or see that your kids don't
fall in the pool. For the halfway stars in Hollywood, life is really
tense. I just can't fit into the Hollywood march. I've never been
able to swing there. All that talk about values and yappety-yap.
Getting up at six, driving out in fog and smog to the studio. All
those people who nibble at you like hungry piranhas. The sluggish-
ness of the studios. Everything overcome by a kind of sleeping sick-
ness. Even in the acting, you think you've done something but it
turns out to be not what you expected. I don't like to go into a
movie unless I can work with the very best director, of my own
choice. Being good in movies is like doing heart surgery. It's great
for some people. The fine thing about Broadway is that if you're
in a hit you can play in it for a year. Even television is better for
an actor than Hollywood movies, especially if you're making a nice,
comfortable series. At least, that way you're steadily employed. However, for myself, I want something more than steady employment
from acting. An important man in one of the big movie studios in
Hollywood once said to me, "You're going to make good pictures
and bad pictures, and if something doesn't come off, we'll just look
at each other and say, 'It's only movies.' " I was shocked. Of course,
some movie producers don't take that attitude at all.

ROBERT PRESTON

After the first blush of enjoyment at seeing myself on the screen, I gradually became more objective about myself. When I'd go to see myself in a movie, it would be almost like watching another actor. Luckily, I've never had a burning desire to exercise absolute control over what I do. Movies are the director's medium and his fun. It's the director who cuts and pastes and makes you come out one way or another. I've heard some directors say, "Give me So-and-So and let me shoot two hundred and fifty thousand feet of film and cut it the way I want to cut it, and *I'll* give you the performance." People in Hollywood still talk about the way John Ford took over Victor McLaglen in "The Informer" and got what he wanted out of that wonderful face. Generally, you have to trust your director, even though you know he makes mistakes. As a movie actor, you really have no choice. Still, it helps in the movies, as well as on the stage, when you work with actors who know exactly what they're doing. I loved working with Gary Cooper. People refer to Cooperisms and Cooper tricks, but I always found him to be a tremendous actor. In "Beau Geste," I was supposed to discover him dead. I was so convinced by his acting that I kept saying, "Speak to me, Coop! Speak to me."

WALTER MATTHAU

In 1953, I made my first movie, "The Kentuckian," in which I portrayed a bad guy with a bullwhip. It was a ridiculous part, and, as with most movie acting, I had no control over the situation; I did it because I was desperately in need of money. Later, I made several movies between plays, including "Bigger Than Life" and "A Face in the Crowd." . . .

It's on the stage that I feel comfortable, relaxed, fulfilled, delighted. I'm happy doing stage plays. Working for the screen is almost like being in the Army; you set your mind to it and you do it. On the stage, you're wide open. There are no tricks with the camera to make you look a certain way. Nobody is going to cut you out, either. The people are sitting out there, and they're going to see you full on. Nobody can fool around with your face. Nobody can fool around with your voice. You can taste and smell what the audience feels. You know if you're coming across. You know if you're being heard. You know if you're being understood. An audience deviates about a yard compared to an actor's performance, which deviates about an inch. An audience of ladies is good if you're in a hit. The critics have told them they have permission to laugh, so they start to laugh before the curtain. They come in laughing at the ushers. Theatre benefits at a comedy make the worst audiences, because people have paid forty-eight dollars for a seat and when you've paid forty-eight dollars for a seat it's hard to laugh. I love to feel I have the whole stage in the palm of my hand. It's what every actor looks for. On the stage, you have a chance to work on a part, and then to work on it some more. Sometimes it takes me six months before I find out what a line means, even if the writing is superficial. Six months after I opened in "Will Success Spoil Rock Hunter?" I stopped seeing the printed page, with all the commas and all the notations. The printed page can remain with you for months and months, until you are experienced enough and relaxed enough to forget it early in the run and make what happens seem to be happening spontaneously.

DIRECTORS

Through Theater to Cinema
by SERGEI EISENSTEIN

It is interesting to retrace the different paths of today's cinema workers to their creative beginnings, which together compose the multi-colored background of the Soviet cinema. In the early 1920s we all came to the Soviet cinema as something not yet existent. We came upon no ready-built city; there were no squares, no streets laid out; not even little crooked lanes and blind alleys, such as we may find in the cinematropolis of our day. We came like bedouins or gold-seekers to a place with unimaginably great possibilities, only a small section of which has even now been developed.

We pitched our tents and dragged into camp our experiences in varied fields. Private activities, accidental past professions, unguessed crafts, unsuspected eruditions—all were pooled and went into the building of something that had, as yet, no written traditions, no exact stylistic requirements, nor even formulated demands.

Without going too far into the theoretical debris of the specifics of cinema, I want here to discuss two of its features. These are features of other arts as well, but the film is particularly accountable to them. *Primo:* photo-fragments of nature are recorded; *secundo:* these fragments are combined in various ways. Thus, the shot (or frame), and thus, montage.

Photography is a system of reproduction to fix real events and elements of actuality. These reproductions, or photo-reflections,

From Film Form, *by Sergei Eisenstein, edited and translated by Jay Leyda. Copyright © 1949 by Harcourt Brace Jovanovich, Inc. Reprinted by permission of Harcourt Brace Jovanovich, Inc.*

may be combined in various ways. Both as reflections and in the manner of their combination, they permit any degree of distortion —either technically unavoidable or deliberately calculated. The results fluctuate from exact naturalistic combinations of visual, interrelated experiences to complete alterations, arrangements unforeseen by nature, and even to abstract formalism, with remnants of reality.

The apparent arbitrariness of matter, in its relation to the *status quo* of nature, is much less arbitrary than it seems. The final order is inevitably determined, consciously or unconsciously, by the social premises of the maker of the film-composition. His class-determined tendency is the basis of what seems to be an arbitrary cinematographic relation to the object placed, or found, before the camera.

We should like to find in this two-fold process (the fragment and its relationships) a hint as to the specifics of cinema, but we cannot deny that this process is to be found in other art mediums, whether close to cinema or not (and which art is not close to cinema?). Nevertheless, it is possible to insist that these features are specific to the film, because film-specifics lie not in the process itself but in the degree to which these features are intensified.

The musician uses a scale of sounds; the painter, a scale of tones; the writer, a row of sounds and words—and these are all taken to an equal degree from nature. But the immutable fragment of actual reality in these cases is narrower and more neutral in meaning, and therefore more flexible in combination, so that when they are put together they lose all visible signs of being combined, appearing as one organic unit. A chord, or even three successive notes, seems to be an organic unit. Why should the combination of three pieces of film in montage be considered as a three-fold collision, as impulses of three successive images?

A blue tone is mixed with a red tone, and the result is thought of as violet, and not as a "double exposure" of red and blue. The same unity of word fragments makes all sorts of expressive variations possible. How easily three shades of meaning can be distinguished in language—for example: "a window without light," "a dark window," and "an unlit window."

Now try to express these various nuances in the composition of the frame. Is it at all possible?

If it is, then what complicated context will be needed in order to string the film-pieces onto the film-thread so that the black shape on the wall will begin to show either as a "dark" or as an "unlit" window? How much wit and ingenuity will be expended in order to reach an effect that words achieve so simply?

The frame is much less independently workable than the word or the sound. Therefore the mutual work of frame and montage is really an enlargement in scale of a process microscopically inherent in all arts. However, in the film this process is raised to such a degree that it seems to acquire a new quality.

The shot, considered as material for the purpose of composition, is more resistant than granite. This resistance is specific to it. The shot's tendency toward complete factual immutability is rooted in its nature. This resistance has largely determined the richness and variety of montage forms and styles—for montage becomes the mightiest means for a really important creative remolding of nature.

Thus the cinema is able, more than any other art, to disclose the process that goes on microscopically in all other arts.

The minimum "distortable" fragment of nature is the shot; ingenuity in its combinations is montage.

Analysis of this problem received the closest attention during the second half-decade of Soviet cinema (1925–1930), an attention often carried to excess. Any infinitesimal alteration of a fact or event before the camera grew, beyond all lawful limit, into whole theories of documentalism. The lawful necessity of combining these fragments of reality grew into montage conceptions which presumed to supplant all other elements of film-expression.

Within normal limits these features enter, as elements, into any style of cinematography. But they are not opposed to nor can they replace other problems—for instance, the problem of *story*.

To return to the double process indicated at the beginning of these notes: if this process is characteristic of cinema, finding its fullest expression during the second stage of Soviet cinema, it will be rewarding to investigate the creative biographies of film-workers of that period, seeing how these features emerged, how they developed in pre-cinema work. All the roads of that period led towards one Rome. I shall try to describe the path that carried me to cinema principles.

Usually my film career is said to have begun with my production of Ostrovsky's play, *Enough Simplicity in Every Sage*, at the Proletcult Theatre (Moscow, March 1923). This is both true and untrue. It is not true if it is based solely on the fact that this production contained a short comic film made especially for it (not separate, but included in the montage plan of the spectacle). It is more nearly true if it is based on the character of the production, for even then the elements of the specifics mentioned above could be detected.

We have agreed that the first sign of a cinema tendency is one showing events with the least distortion, aiming at the factual reality of the fragments.

A search in this direction shows my film tendencies beginning three years earlier, in the production of *The Mexican* (from Jack London's story). Here, my participation brought into the theater "events" themselves—a purely cinematographic element, as distinguished from "reactions to events"—which is a purely theatrical element.

This is the plot: A Mexican revolutionary group needs money for its activities. A boy, a Mexican, offers to find the money. He trains for boxing, and contracts to let the champion beat him for a fraction of the prize. Instead he beats up the champion, winning the entire prize. Now that I am better acquainted with the specifics of the Mexican revolutionary struggle, not to mention the technique of boxing, I would not think of interpreting this material as we did in 1920, let alone using so unconvincing a plot.

The play's climax is the prize-fight. In accordance with the most hallowed Art Theatre traditions, this was to take place backstage (like the bull-fight in *Carmen*), while the actors on stage were to show excitement in the fight only they can see, as well as to portray the various emotions of the persons concerned in the outcome.

My first move (trespassing upon the director's job, since I was there in the official capacity of designer only) was to propose that the fight be brought into view. Moreover I suggested that the scene be staged in the center of the auditorium to re-create the same circumstances under which a real boxing match takes place. Thus we dared the concreteness of factual events. The fight was to be carefully planned in advance but was to be utterly realistic.

The playing of our young worker-actors in the fight scene differed radically from their acting elsewhere in the production. In every other scene, one emotion gave rise to a further emotion (they were working in the Stanislavsky system), which in turn was used as a means to affect the audience; but in the fight scene the audience was excited directly.

While the other scenes influenced the audience through intonation, gestures, and mimicry, our scene employed realistic, even textural means—real fighting, bodies crashing to the ring floor, panting, the shine of sweat on torsos, and finally, the unforgettable smacking of gloves against taut skin and strained muscles. Illusionary scenery gave way to a realistic ring (though not in the center of the hall, thanks to that plague of every theatrical enterprise, the fireman) and extras closed the circle around the ring.

Thus my realization that I had struck new ore, an actual-materialistic element in theater. In *The Sage,* this element appeared on a new and clearer level. The eccentricity of the production exposed this same line, through fantastic contrasts. The tendency developed not only from illusionary acting movement, but from the physical fact of acrobatics. A gesture expands into gymnastics, rage is expressed through a somersault, exaltation through a *salto-mortale,* lyricism on "the mast of death." The grotesque of this style permitted leaps from one type of expression to another, as well as unexpected intertwinings of the two expressions. In a later production, *Listen, Moscow* (summer 1923), these two separate lines of "real doing" and "pictorial imagination" went through a synthesis expressed in a specific technique of acting.

These two principles appeared again in Tretiakov's *Gas Masks* (1923–24), with still sharper irreconcilability, broken so noticeably that had this been a film it would have remained, as we say, "on the shelf."

What was the matter? The conflict between material-practical and fictitious-descriptive principles was somehow patched up in the melodrama, but here they broke up and we failed completely. The cart dropped to pieces, and its driver dropped into the cinema.

This all happened because one day the director had the marvelous idea of producing this play about a gas factory—in a real gas factory.

As we realized later, the real interiors of the factory had nothing to do with our theatrical fiction. At the same time the plastic charm of reality in the factory became so strong that the element of acuality rose with fresh strength—took things into its own hands—and finally had to leave an art where it could not command.

Thereby bringing us to the brink of cinema.

But this is not the end of our adventures with theater work. Having come to the screen, this other tendency flourished, and became known as "typage." This "typage" is just as typical a feature of this cinema period as "montage." And be it known that I do not want to limit the concept of "typage" or "montage" to my own works.

I want to point out that "typage" must be understood as broader than merely a face without make-up, or a substitution of "naturally expressive" types for actors. In my opinion, "typage" included a specific approach to the events embraced by the content of the film. Here again was the method of least interference with the natural course and combinations of events. In concept, from beginning to end, *October* is pure "typage."

A typage tendency may be rooted in theater; growing out of the theater into film, it presents possibilities for excellent stylistic growth, in a broad sense—as an indicator of definite affinities to real life through the camera.[1]

---

[1] Eisenstein has said that one might define typage as a modern development of the *Commedia dell'arte*—with its seven stock figures multiplied into infinity. The relationship lies not in numbers, but in audience conditioning. Upon entrance of Pantalone or the Captain, his mask tells the audience immediately what to expect of this figure. Modern film typage is based on the need for presenting each new figure in our first glimpse of him so sharply and completely that further use of this figure may be as a known element. Thus new, immediate conventions are created.—J.L.

And now let us examine the second feature of film-specifics, the principles of montage. How was this expressed and shaped in my work before joining the cinema?

In the midst of the flood of eccentricity in *The Sage,* including a short film comedy, we can find the first hints of a sharply expressed montage.

The action moves through an elaborate tissue of intrigue. Mamayev sends his nephew, Glumov, to his wife as guardian. Glumov takes liberties beyond his uncle's instructions and his aunt takes the courtship seriously. At the same time Glumov begins to negotiate for a marriage with Mamayev's niece, Turussina, but conceals these intentions from the aunt, Mamayeva. Courting the aunt, Glumov deceives the uncle; flattering the uncle, Glumov arranges with him the deception of the aunt.

Glumov, on a comic plane, echoes the situations, the overwhelming passions, the thunder of finance, that his French prototype, Balzac's Rastignac, experiences. Rastignac's type in Russia was still in the cradle. Money-making was still a sort of child's game between uncles and nephews, aunts and their gallants. It remains in the family, and remains trivial. Hence, the comedy. But the intrigue and entanglements are already present, playing on two fronts at the same time—with both hands—with dual characters . . . and we showed all this with an intertwined montage of two different scenes (of Mamayev giving his instructions, and of Glumov putting them into execution). The surprising intersections of the two dialogues sharpen the characters and the play, quicken the tempo, and multiply the comic possibilities.

For the production of *The Sage* the stage was shaped like a circus arena, edged with a red barrier, and three-quarters surrounded by the audience. The other quarter was hung with a striped curtain, in front of which stood a small raised platform, several steps high. The scene with Mamayev (Shtraukh) took place downstage while the Mamayeva (Yanukova) fragments occurred on the platform. Instead of changing scenes, Glumov (Yezikanov) ran from one scene to the other and back—taking a fragment of dialogue from one scene, interrupting it with a fragment from the other scene—the dialogue thus colliding, creating new meanings and sometimes word-plays. Glumov's leaps acted as *caesurae* between the dialogue fragments.

And the "cutting" increased in tempo. What was most interesting was that the extreme sharpness of the eccentricity was not torn from the context of this part of the play; it never became comical just for comedy's sake, but stuck to its theme, sharpened by its scenic embodiment.

Another distinct film feature at work here was the new meaning acquired by common phrases in a new environment.

Everyone who has had in his hands a piece of film to be edited knows by experience how neutral it remains, even though a part of a planned sequence, until it is joined with another piece, when it suddenly acquires and conveys a sharper and quite different meaning than that planned for it at the time of filming.

This was the foundation of that wise and wicked art of reediting the work of others, the most profound examples of which can be found during the dawn of our cinematography, when all the master film-editors—Esther Schub,[2] the Vassiliyev brothers, Benjamin Boitler, and Birrois—were engaged in reworking ingeniously the films imported after the revolution.

I cannot resist the pleasure of citing here one montage *tour de force* of this sort, executed by Boitler. One film bought from Germany was *Danton*, with Emil Jannings. As released on our screens, this scene was shown: Camille Desmoulins is condemned to the guillotine. Greatly agitated, Danton rushes to Robespierre, who turns aside and slowly wipes away a tear. The sub-title said, approximately, "In the name of freedom I had to sacrifice a friend. . . ." Fine.

But who could have guessed that in the German original, Danton, represented as an idler, a petticoat-chaser, a splendid chap and the only positive figure in the midst of evil characters, that this Danton

---

2 Schub, long a familiar name to world-documentalists, is known abroad only by the film exhibited in America as *Cannons and Tractors*. The first time Eisenstein ever joined together two pieces of "real film" was while assisting Esther Schub in the re-editing of Lang's *Dr. Mabuse*. This was shortly after the production of *The Sage*. The Vassiliyevs' *Chapayev* establishes their place in cinema history.—J. L.

ran to the evil Robespierre and . . . spat in his face? And that it
was this spit that Robespierre wiped from his face with a handker-
chief? And that the title indicated Robespierre's hatred of Danton,
a hate that in the end of the film motivates the condemnation of
Jannings-Danton to the guillotine?!

Two tiny cuts reversed the entire significance of this scene!

Where did my montage experiment in these scenes of *The Sage*
come from?

There was already an "aroma" of montage in the new "left"
cinema, particularly among the documentalists. Our replacement
of Glumov's diary in Ostrovsky's text with a short "film-diary" was
itself a parody on the first experiments with newsreels.

I think that first and foremost we must give the credit to the basic
principles of the circus and the music-hall—for which I had had
a passionate love since childhood. Under the influence of the French
comedians, and of Chaplin (of whom we had only heard), and the
first news of the fox-trot and jazz, this early love thrived.

The music-hall element was obviously needed at the time for
the emergence of a "montage" form of thought. Harlequin's parti-
colored costume grew and spread, first over the structure of the
program, and finally into the method of the whole production.

But the background extended more deeply into tradition.
Strangely enough, it was Flaubert who gave us one of the finest
examples of cross-montage of dialogues, used with the same intention of expressive sharpening of idea. This is the scene in *Madame
Bovary* where Emma and Rodolphe grow more intimate. Two lines
of speech are interlaced: the speech of the orator in the square
below, and the conversation of the future lovers:

> Monsieur Derozerays got up, beginning another speech . . .
> praise of the Government took up less space in it; religion and
> agriculture more. He showed in it the relations of these two, and
> how they had always contributed to civilization. Rodolphe with
> Madame Bovary was talking dreams, presentiments, magnetism.
> Going back to the cradle of society, the orator painted those fierce
> times when men lived on acorns in the heart of woods. Then they

had left off the skins of beasts, had put on cloth, tilled the soil, planted the vine. Was this a good, and in this discovery was there not more of injury than of gain? Monsieur Derozerays set himself this problem. From magnetism little by little Rodolphe had come to affinities, and while the president was citing Cincinnatus and his plough, Diocletian planting his cabbages, and the Emperors of China inaugurating the year by the sowing of seed, the young man was explaining to the young woman that these irresistible attractions find their cause in some previous state of experience.

"Thus we," he said, "why did we come to know one another? What chance willed it? It was because across the infinite, like two streams that flow but to unite, our special bents of mind had driven us towards each other."

And he seized her hand; she did not withdraw it.

"For good farming generally!" cried the president.

"Just now, for example, when I went to your house."

"To Monsieur Bizat of Quincampoix."

"Did I know I should accompany you?"

"Seventy francs."

"A hundred times I wished to go; and I followed you—I remained."

"Manures!"

"And I shall remain to-night, to-morrow, all other days, all my life!"

And so on, with the "pieces" developing increasing tension.

As we can see, this is an interweaving of two lines, thematically identical, equally trivial. The matter is sublimated to a monumental triviality, whose climax is reached through a continuation of this cross-cutting and word-play, with the significance always dependent on the juxtaposition of the two lines.

Literature is full of such examples. This method is used with increasing popularity by Flaubert's artistic heirs.

Our pranks in regard to Ostrovsky remained on an "avant garde" level of an indubitable nakedness. But this seed of montage tendencies grew quickly and splendidly in *Patatra,* which remained a project through lack of an adequate hall and technical possibilities. The production was planned with "chase tempos," quick changes of action, scene intersections, and simultaneous playing of several scenes on a stage that surrounded an auditorium of revolving seats. Another even earlier project attempted to embrace the entire theater building in its composition. This was broken up during rehearsals and later produced by other hands as a purely theatrical conception. It was the Pletnëv play, *Precipice,* which Smishlayev and I worked on, following *The Mexican,* until we disagreed on principles and dissolved our partnership. (When I returned to Proletcult a year later, to do *The Sage,* it was as a director, although I continued to design my own productions.)

Precipice contains a scene where an inventor, thrilled by his new invention, runs, like Archimedes, about the city (or perhaps he was being chased by gangsters—I don't remember exactly). The task was to solve the dynamics of city streets, as well as to show the helplessness of an individual at the mercy of the "big city." (Our mistaken imaginings about Europe naturally led us to the false concept of "urbanism.")

An amusing combination occurred to me, not only to use running scenery—pieces of buildings and details (Meyerhold had not yet worked out, for his *Trust D. E.,* the neutral polished shields, *murs mobiles,* to unify several places of action)—but also, possibly under the demands of shifting scenery, to connect these moving decorations with people. The actors on roller skates carried not only themselves about the stage, but also their "piece of city." Our solution of the problem—the intersection of man and milieu—was undoubtedly influenced by the principles of the cubists. But the "urbanistic" paintings of Picasso were of less importance here than the need to express the dynamics of the city—glimpses of façades, hands, legs, pillars, heads, domes. All of this can be found in Gogol's work, but we did not notice that until Andrei Belyi enlightened us about the special cubism of Gogol. I still remember the four legs of two bankers, supporting the façade of the stock-exchange, with two top-hats crowning the whole. There was also a policeman, sliced and quartered with traffic. Costumes blazing with perspectives of twirling lights, with only great rouged lips visible above. These all remained on paper—and now that even the paper has gone, we may become quite pathetically lyrical in our reminiscences.

These close-ups cut into views of a city become another link in our analysis, a film element that tried to fit itself into the stubborn stage. Here are also elements of double and multiple exposure—"superimposing" images of man onto images of buildings—all an attempt to interrelate man and his milieu in a single complicated display. (The fact that the film *Strike* was full of this sort of complexity proves the "infantile malady of leftism" existing in these first steps of cinema.)

Out of mechanical fusion, from plastic synthesis, the attempt evolves into thematic synthesis. In *Strike,* there is more than a transformation into the technique of the camera. The composition and structure of the film as a whole achieves the effect and sensation of uninterrupted unity between the collective and the milieu that creates the collective. And the organic unity of sailors, battleships, and sea that is shown in plastic and thematic cross-section in *Potemkin* is not by trickery or double-exposure or mechanical intersection, but by the general structure of the composition. But in the theater, the impossibility of the *mise-en-scène* unfolding throughout the auditorium, fusing stage and audience in a developing pattern, was the reason for the concentrated absorption of the *mise-en-scène* problems within the scenic action.

The almost geometrically conventional *mise-en-scène* of *The Sage* and its formal sequel, *Listen, Moscow,* becomes one of the basic elements of expression. The montage intersection eventually became too emphatically exact. The composition singled out groups, shifted the spectator's attention from one point to another, presented close-ups, a hand holding a letter, the play of eyebrows, a glance. The technique of genuine *mise-en-scène* composition was being mastered—and approaching its limits. It was already threatened with becoming the knight's move in chess, the shift of purely plastic contours in the already non-theatrical outlines of detailed drawings.

Sculptural details seen through the frame of the *cadre,* or shot, transitions from shot to shot, appeared to be the logical way out for the threatened hypertrophy of the *mise-en-scène*. Theoretically it established our dependence on *mise-en-scène* and montage. Pedagogically, it determined, for the future, the approaches to montage and cinema, arrived at through the mastering of theatrical construction and through the art of *mise-en-scène*.[3] Thus was born the concept of *mise-en-cadre*. As the *mise-en-scène* is an interrelation of people in action, so the *mise-en-cadre* is the pictorial composition of mutually dependent *cadres* (shots) in a montage sequence.

In *Gas Masks* we see all the elements of film tendencies meeting. The turbines, the factory background, negated the last remnants of make-up and theatrical costumes, and all elements appeared as independently fused. Theater accessories in the midst of real factory plastics appeared ridiculous. The element of "play" was incompatible with the acrid smell of gas. The pitiful platform kept getting lost among the real platforms of labor activity. In short, the production was a failure. And we found ourselves in the cinema.

Our first film opus, *Strike* [1924–25], reflected, as in a mirror, in reverse, our production of *Gas Masks*. But the film floundered about in the flotsam of a rank theatricality that had become alien to it.

At the same time, the break with the theater in principle was so sharp that in my "revolt against the theater" I did away with a very vital element of theater—the story.

At that time this seemed natural. We brought collective and mass action onto the screen, in contrast to individualism and the "triangle" drama of the bourgeois cinema. Discarding the individualist conception of the bourgeois hero, our films of this period made an abrupt deviation—insisting on an understanding of the mass as hero.

No screen had ever before reflected an image of collective action. Now the conception of "collectivity" was to be pictured. But our enthusiasm produced a one-sided representation of the masses and the collective; one-sided because collectivism means the maximum development of the individual within the collective, a conception irreconcilably opposed to bourgeois individualism. Our first mass films missed this deeper meaning.

Still, I am sure that for its period this deviation was not only natural but necessary. It was important that the screen be first pene-

[3] As indicated in "A Course in Treatment," the first two years of Eisenstein's course for directors at the State Cinema Institute emphasize a thorough study of *theater* principles.—J. L.

trated by the general image, the collective united and propelled by one wish. "Individuality within the collective," the deeper meaning, demanded of cinema today, would have found entrance almost impossible if the way had not been cleared by the general concept.

In 1924 I wrote, with intense zeal: "Down with the story and the plot!" Today, the story, which then seemed to be almost "an attack of individualism" upon our revolutionary cinema, returns in a fresh form, to its proper place. In this turn towards the story lies the historical importance of the third half-decade of Soviet cinematography (1930–1935).

And here, as we begin our fourth five-year period of cinema, when abstract discussions of the epigones of the "story" film and the embryones of the "plotless" film are calming down, it is time to take an inventory of our credits and debits.

I consider that besides mastering the elements of filmic diction, the technique of the frame, and the theory of montage, we have another credit to list—the value of profound ties with the traditions and methodology of literature. Not in vain, during this period, was the new concept of film-language born, film-language not as the language of the film-critic, but as an expression of cinema thinking, when the cinema was called upon to embody the philosophy and ideology of the victorious proletariat.

Stretching out its hand to the new quality of literature—the dramatics of subject—the cinema cannot forget the tremendous experience of its earlier periods. But the way is not back to them, but forward to the synthesis of all the best that has been done by our silent cinematography, towards a synthesis of these with the demands of today, along the lines of story and Marxist-Leninist ideological analysis. The phase of monumental synthesis in the images of the people of the epoch of socialism—the phase of socialist realism.

Interview with Elia Kazan
by BERNARD R. KANTOR, IRWIN R. BLACKER, AND ANNE KRAMER

Elia Kazan was interviewed in a small walkup office on Broadway in New York City. It would be difficult to find a greater contrast to the Hollywood suite he would warrant than this writer-producer-director's working office. A warm personality who had about him none of the trappings that usually adorn the presence of the "important man," Kazan seemed to be deeply involved in what he was doing and how he was doing it. Too old now to question the *why* —he had already made up his mind about that.

In New York Kazan is a writer-at-work and not a director, but his own strong feelings about himself and his work as a film director dominate most of his thinking. Outside the office the noise of New York traffic, news vendors, and the confusion of the city seemed to press in on a visitor, but Kazan did not seem to be aware of the sounds. Several times the interview was interrupted by phone calls —someone wanting a job, someone wanting to offer a job, several personal messages.

The actor still appears when Kazan moves with a grace that belies his years, and there seems to be about him the lightness of a fighter on his feet, ready to weave and shift. Even in the simple background of his office, he gives an interviewer the impression of a committed man who is as much fighter as artist.

Question: Let's go back to the beginning. You started in theater. How did that happen?

Kazan: The thing that brought me into the theater was, oddly enough, films by Eisenstein and Dovzhenko that I saw in the early thirties. They made a profound impression on me. So before I was ever in the theater I wanted above all to be a film director.

It was impossible in those days, or I felt it was, to say, "I'm going to be a film director," and start becoming one. So when I got a chance to go with The Group Theater I jumped at it. There I met two men, Harold Clurman and Lee Strasberg, who did the same thing that the Eisenstein and Dovzhenko films did: made me feel that the performing arts, theater and film, can be as meaningful as the drama of living itself. And they made the theater, which was at that time in New York just a way to kill time, seem relevant to the social events of the time.

I was taken into The Group Theater, was a stage manager for a while, then an actor. But always in the back of my head what I *finally* wanted was to be a film director. During my early years with The Group Theater I did make a couple of documentary films, one with a man named Ralph Steiner. He and I and another actor went out to the city dump, and improvised a two-reel comedy that was great fun to do. Then I did a documentary for an outfit called Frontier Films that——

Question: Was that the agriculture film?

Kazan: No, it was about coal miners in northeastern Tennessee. It was called *People of the Cumberlands.* I think my experience there, photographing non-enacted drama—day-to-day living behavior— was influential on the work I did later. I've always known since that I could go into any environment and not only find interesting faces and people, but the drama and the poetry the simplest people have. What's poetic and what isn't, what's dramatic and what isn't, is in the eyes of the beholder, of course. Just being among these people with a camera was itself a dramatic event. It was a small camera and we didn't know exactly what we were going to do every morning, simply went out and photographed what we saw that interested us. That for me was the beginning of what critics call neo-realism. That experience showed me that before and beyond a script there was life itself to photograph.

Question: So story—script—has always been secondary for you?

Kazan: No, I'm a great believer in having a well-constructed story. Story is the way character and destiny work themselves out in the lives of people. I like to watch a progression, one event influencing the next, and so on till the final climax. That's the way I feel life myself. What we do today is never erased; it determines what we do tomorrow. I believe in script too, and I've always worked very hard on mine. At the same time I always try to leave the script free enough, open enough so that the human material that's being photographed is not rigidly arranged to the point of choking out surprises, any unexpected possibilities. I think when you simply write a script, then photograph it mechanically, it is economically the practical thing to do and saves a great deal of money, but I think there's often a great deal lost. The process of shooting a film should be a creative one, not just a recording of what has already been determined before the shooting itself starts.

Question: Do you think that your original acting experience in things like *Golden Boy* and *Night Music* has or did have a great deal to do with your working with actors?

Kazan: I suppose so. I like actors and have great respect for the difficulties of their profession. I joke about it and say that the fact that I was an actor made me not afraid of actors. But it's more than that reality. Perhaps I understand their potentialities more having been one of them, and this allows me to use their creativity. In other words I don't—perhaps because I was an actor—insist on a single interpretation. I somehow try to get them going and allow their own imaginations and their own reactions to the material to express itself. With a very good actor especially, I play for surprises. I set little traps and hope that he or she will do something that's better than what I had preconceived. In the case of the very best actors the most gratifying thing about working with them is that they not only perform what I had in mind, they go further; they improve on what I had in mind, and very often they reveal things about the material that I had not imagined and for which I feel very grateful. "My God," I feel, "I could never have anticipated that!" or "Look what he's doing that I never knew was in this."

Question: Do you think the Actors Studio which you founded has something to do with this? And the Method?

Kazan: "The Method"—that term—has become a columnist's joke. There are an awful lot of people who make teaching the Method a racket today and it's a very good living. Actually the Method was two quite different things: one, a method of training actors, and the other, a method of rehearsing. It was never, as I understood it, a method of acting, but a way of training that takes many years. It's very hard work and requires tremendous devotion. The other thing is that it's a method of rehearsing a play or preparing a production of a play. The great Russian stage directors used this "method" very well; that is, they would go on the premise that rehearsal is a process, subtle, often long, a little mysterious. They scorned easy definitions and oversimplifications. For them the "method" was neither a panacea nor a quick, all-purpose stage trick or instant culture for sale.

Question: In terms of working as a director both in theater and films, particularly with the Williams plays and the Miller plays, what specifically did you do in terms of adaptation from the stage to the film?

Kazan: I only did one——

Question: I'm thinking of *Streetcar.*

Kazan: I only did one piece of work in both mediums. I had tremendous respect for *Streetcar Named Desire* and for Williams himself, and I still do, no less than I've ever had. I think he's *the* best playwright we've had in my time. When I started to make a film of that play, I thought in the usual terms. I thought we'd better open the play up, move it around a bit, make it pictorially more varied and so on. After all, I thought, film is a visual medium. We had better play some of the scenes somewhere else. So I worked with a writer for about seven or eight months on an "opened-up" script. I thought it was pretty good, put it away for a few days, then read it again, and found it a total loss. I realized the compression in *Streetcar* is its strength. So I went back and photographed the stage play as written. I think that particular play merited that treatment and I thought the film came off pretty well.

Question: In terms of your own adaptations and stories, you've really worked very closely with writers, haven't you?

Kazan: Yes, I have. I started working very closely with writers in 1952 when I did *Viva Zapata!* with John Steinbeck. Of course, that's his work, and he did a tremendous amount of research and knew just about everything on the subject. But I worked very closely with him and I've worked very closely with every author since. Most of the things I've done, or that I did up until 1963—in that eleven-year period—were projects I initiated. I would suggest to an author, "Why don't we do this together?" Or, an author and I would get to talking and say, "Why don't we make a film out of this?" Then I would work closely with him. That doesn't mean I wrote the material. I did not. But I worked on the premise that I would be telling a good part of the story through the images I chose. It was understood without any declarations or anything of that kind that, since the story was going to be told through the camera, it was important that I be involved in the arrangement of scenes and sequences, as well as the images and the way the film was finally going to be cut. So I did work very closely with writers; nearly all good directors do. In 1963, however, I wanted to make films from stories that meant more to me personally, that were out of my personal past, or out of my own life experience. I wrote a script myself, an original screenplay called *America, America,* and I made that. Many people who've seen that picture feel that I would have done it better if I'd had a collaborator of some kind or a producer to tell me it was a bit long, and so on. But I don't feel that way. I think it is a little long, but all in all I was pleased with it and happy that I'd been able to do it. And, more important for me, I felt a great opening up of possibilities. Having had a taste of writing, I decided to write more, and I wrote a novel called *The Arrangement,* and am about to film it.

Question: You did your own screenplay?

Kazan: I had an interesting experience with that. It took me about a year to write the first draft of the novel. It's quite a personal novel. It's not autobiographical, but still, in one way or another I've experienced most of what's there or people I've been very close to have. So when it came time to do the screenplay I found that I had to do it. I could not get someone else to adapt it, even though I'd have liked that. And I could not use most of the material in the novel. So in effect I wrote an original screenplay which I'm now going to film. I had to retell the story entirely. I've never had such a sense of the difference between a literary work and a work that is essentially communicated by visual images as I had doing this job.

It was a shock to me. I started thinking, "Well, after all, I'm a film-maker. I wrote a novel and it must be just a matter of picking a bit here and a bit there to tell the same story." But I couldn't do that. I tried but it was cumbersome and vastly overlength, and it was formless. I had to throw it away and start on an entirely fresh tack. I think I've got an interesting screenplay now, but it's the same story told in an entirely different way.

Question: Does the film grow out of Eddie's mind and body as much as the action of the book did?

Kazan: Well, I haven't shot it yet, so I'd rather not talk too much about it, but there is a lot of it presented as Eddie sees it; you are in his mind a lot. The luxury of writing a novel is that you can go into things and take off from things; the best parts of my book I thought were flights of thought, reflections and comments that I made on the scene around us. Those are the parts that I like best. But in a film, one quick image will often do it.

Question: One quick image!

Kazan: Yes. There's something magical about film. It's so elliptical, so much a matter of suggestion. And the vocabulary of film has developed so. Often it's better *not* to make things too clear, better to leave areas of mystery where an audience is tantalized or roused to thought and feelings of its own. All art is a shared experience. But particularly film. Whereas in a novel you're usually saying, "Here's how I see things and how I think and I'm going to convince you that you must think or feel the same way," in a film it's quicksilver. You see a fish in the sea, it's there, then it's gone! One fault with *America, America* was that it was too explicit, too clear, therefore often redundant. I will try in this film to move more quickly and more elliptically.

Question: It seems to me that in recent film there has been a great deal more complexity in human relationships. Do you think that that has had any influence on you?

Kazan: Yes, I've been very influenced and I've been very moved by the new film-makers—I don't mean just the interest in style that the French are so devoted to, I mean all of them, the Japanese, the Italians, the English, and the great Swede, and Ray in India, and now Rocha in South America. All over the world something wonderful has been happening, particularly in the last ten years. The whole vocabulary and idiom of film-making has come alive and is still expanding. I admire many of the younger men, those who haven't quite come out yet. They are exhausting every possibility in every direction, proving that artistic habits are only a rigidity of mind and must be broken. This is going on in every art form, of course, but the theater and films, till recently, were behind. Now films are the vanguard. These new film-makers have taken something that was *locked* in the American film tradition and opened it up. So all of us are much freer now in our use of techniques. We are here-and-now finding, as the rest of the world already has found, that we are just beginning to realize the potentials of this marvelous medium.

Question: Will you be doing that kind of thing in your next picture?

Kazan: I don't understand.

Question: Jump-cutting, subliminal shots——?

Kazan: Jump-cutting and that kind of thing—those are just the externals. It's the whole attitude toward the material of films and the techniques of film that have changed. For one thing, film-makers are more aware of the dangers of overordering material. The danger in the kind of structure that by oversimplifying takes the contradictions and the poetry out of life. And we've become very leery of oversimplified messages too. I am wary of the man who is rigid in his viewpoint, a man who says to me, "You must think as I do. I'll tell you how you should think." We've messed up the world so badly that everyone is understandably very careful of the simplifications—political, social, or moral—of ten and twenty years ago. If a man preaches at me and says, "This is the conclusion you must come to from this material," when I feel that heavy hand on me, his cold moral fingers at my throat, I shake him off. I say, "Go preach at someone else." I believe that we are now attempting to find truths without robbing life of its contradictory elements and its complexities.

Question: What about the kind of thing that's going on now in terms of "There should be no more violent films"?

Kazan: A film that makes entertainment out of smashing a person's face in, or says that brutality is fun, and killing is sport, is reprehensible. That doesn't mean I think all films should say how wonderful things are; they're not. It depends not on whether there's violence or not but on the basic use to which the images of violence are put. If the purpose is genuine, if a point has to be made through tremendous violence, I'm all for it. The thing is, to tell the truth. The film that reflects the violence that's now going on in this country truly and honestly has great value.

Question: Do you think that the film-maker, the creative artist, has an obligation to make a film about something that he believes in?

Kazan: An obligation? He just does. You see, the thing about Hollywood is that it was basically organized, and is today still basically organized as an industry. No matter what you say about what a film contains, its artistic aspects and so on, the purpose of the people who put up money is to make more money. Quick. It's too bad that an art is used that way. The purpose of art is to make man confront his humanity. That's a very complex thing, and a very difficult thing. The large studios call themselves industries, and they're right. They are industries, and an industry is a profit-making effort first and always. Every year the people who head big studios get up and make speeches to their shareholders and tell what their profits were, as if that was the sole purpose of their efforts. And they're quite right. But that doesn't mean that that is the highest purpose to which this art should be put. That's why I think another great thing that's happening today is that there are other ways of making films, less expensive, therefore freer. After all, finally, film-making is a very simple thing. It's just a camera and an environment and the people around this environment and the drama that the film-maker sees.

Question: Do you think that in terms of technology, just to get back to the big studios for a minute, that they will allow the kind of innovations that we really should be having in terms of camera, equipment, etc.?

Kazan: I don't give a damn if they allow them or not; people are doing them anyway. The big studios got rattled a few years ago over the huge profits that some of the foreign films were making and how badly our films were doing. So they began to loosen up on their code of morality. Suddenly there was more nudity, more candor, and more freedom in subject matter. But the impulse to do all that was not to free the medium and the art; the impulse was born when the front-office fellows saw there were profits to be made that way and, of course, they grabbed at that. If there is more enlightenment today, it's basically because the industry was shaken up.

Question: Well, you've worked for all the major studios, but always for yourself, as producer, director, and writer. Do you feel you've ever had problems coping with the industry?

Kazan: Oh yes, but I think the biggest difficulty an artist has or that a worker in the arts has is in dealing with himself. Those are the really subtle difficulties. I have no real complaints about the people that run the studios. By their measures they've been fair to me and sometimes very generous. I like a lot of them and I don't complain about them. It's just that their goal, their aim, is a different one than my own. I don't want to go into this because I am in no mood to complain about anybody. I feel very happy and not grumpy a bit.

Question: So then you feel hopeful?

Kazan: Yes. The great hope is that with faster film stock, with much lighter equipment, with much less equipment necessary, with film-makers who like to write, produce, and direct their own films (in fact, it's really one process) we are returning to a simplicity of working in the medium. I wish there was some way of getting the money necessary for films without going to the big companies. But even this is beginning to happen and in time——

Question: What about the Hollywood unions? Do you think they can be handled so you can work with lighter crews?

Kazan: I don't really know; I haven't made a film in Hollywood for many years. When I go to visit one of the big studios, I know a lot of the fellows who work there and I understand their problem. It's simple—they *should* be assured a yearly wage. They have to be protected that way, and they're right to protect themselves. On the other hand, I think the solution of just saying, "You must have so and so many crew members on every picture," is a preposterous one. I think we're going to have to meet, in one way or another, the industry, the unions, everybody, the new circumstances. I remember one day I was making a film and we were out on location, and all we were doing were a few modest shots of two people talking. Very few lights were needed. I looked behind me and I saw over a hundred men, the crew, all sitting there doing nothing, and they were all on my picture. That picture cost far more than it should have. I think the unions will have to be doing something about that. But I can't answer the problem organizationally. I last made a film in California in 1955.

Question: Is there a specific reason for not having made a film— because of your novel, or———?

Kazan: Between 1962 and 1964 I worked in Lincoln Center, then I wrote my novel, then the screenplay of it, and I'm writing another book now. I decided to write on my own, so I've stopped making so many films.

Question: It's a totally different way of living, isn't it?

Kazan: I like that part of it, because you're essentially living within yourself. You're not responding to pressures: "Do you like this story? Do you want to make a film of this play? Answer me immediately! Here's a great novel, read it right away, it would make a good film!" You're not doing that. Instead you're thinking, "What do *I* want to say." You know when you're fifty-eight you shouldn't live the way you lived when you were thirty-eight. When I was thirty-eight, I was doing plays and movies, two or three a year; I never stopped working. But now I've reached the point in my life when I just want to do the few things I really want to do, and that's the way I try to live.

Question: Do you find there is a different kind of feeling in terms of working in films and theater and writing? They are three totally different kinds of activities.

Kazan: Oh, yes. As I said, when you're writing a novel, you're living within yourself. You have difficulties, but they're of your own making. You have limitations, but they're your own limitations, not organizational ones. I live in the country a lot, which is an entirely different way of living. I love privacy, to be by myself a part of every day, and I like working on my own material. When you've produced a book and you hold the damn thing in your hand and think, "That's all out of me!" it's like a woman feels with a child, I suppose.

Question: And as for critical reaction, how does that compare?

Kazan: You don't really give a damn. You *hope* people will like it, but deep down you don't give a damn. Some of the critics and some of my friends didn't like my book, *The Arrangement.* Of course I wished they had, but it didn't bother me too much. I feel what it contains is the truth; it was, one way or another, lived through by me and I put it down as truthfully as I could. Something you do yourself is valid for you whether it is successful for others or not. When you work in theater or in films, directing a play or dramatizing a novel, you are a steward for someone else, you're hoping that Tennessee Williams or Arthur Miller will like what you do and that you're bringing their play off for the public and expressing what they, your authors, feel, being true to them. In the theater you must hope that this whole group that's collected around you is successful as a group, that you've brought their efforts to a successful conclusion. But when you write a novel, you look at it finally and say, "Well, for better or worse, that's me," and so you've got something that's much more satisfying and, in a way, invulnerable. I expect I'll have the same feeling about the films I do from my works. I did about *America, America.* I realize it had serious faults, people pointed them out to me, but I really didn't give a damn, I was so proud of it. I'm more proud of it than any film I ever did. *The Arrangement* means more to me than anything I ever did. And it has nothing to do with other people's reactions to it. As I say, when you're sixty, you begin to look inside yourself and ask, "Well, who am I really and what am I like? What do I feel? What do I prize? What do I hate? What do I want to change? What is the way I want to live? Whom do I love?" And you begin to think that way. And when you write your book you have the luxury of living entirely with yourself which is a great and deep feeling. Well, you see, there are people who make films in Europe in this way—Fellini, and Ray in India, Bergman. Oh, a lot of others. There are a lot of film-makers in England, in France, and in Italy who——

Question: Do you like Bergman's work?

Kazan: Yes, I do. Every film is a piece of his autobiography. That's what I like about his work. It's oblique and subtle and personally seen; you can't quite put your finger on it, but it's a piece of him. He's a true artist. I think Fellini is, too. In *8 1/2* there is a scene I will never forget: the one in which the hero imagines his wife and his mistress dancing together among the cafe tables. Every man's dream of "Why can't my wife love my mistress? Why can't my mistress love my wife? Why can't they like each other and get along together."

Question: But let's just jump back to *The Arrangement.* How do you feel about casting someone as yourself?

Kazan: I don't think of that part—Eddie Anderson—as myself. Not at all. It's like some of my friends, yes, and I've had some of the experiences he's had, yes, but I'm not like that. The basic thing about Eddie in *The Arrangement* is that he's finally and totally dissatisfied with his life. I've never been unhappy about what I've been doing. I've always wanted to be a director, I've always wanted to be an artist, I've always felt myself lucky to be able to work in the theater, and in films, and now as a writer. If I was unhappy for any length of time with what I was doing, I changed it. I've never been miserable and I've never been suicidal. I've always been basically a happy person because I've always functioned in the area that I wanted to function in. Eddie hates himself; he's full of self-scorn and self-disgust. I've done wrong, but I've never been full of self-disgust. So when you say, "it's like you," you're wrong; it's not. It's like a lot of people I've known, and it's like a lot of people around me. Symbolically you can say it's like America now, in the middle of its course and not knowing what's gone wrong or where to turn next. I thought it had those overtones.

Question: Will you direct the film?

Kazan: Oh, yes.

Question: Will you produce it alone?

Kazan: I'm producer, director, writer, and I sweep the stage.

Question: The whole thing.

Kazan: The whole thing.

Question: What about the end?

Kazan: Well, I've got a different end. I think it's rather good. It has the same qualities as the old end. I've managed to keep the last sentence of the book—the one people remember most—tried to keep it and make it valid in the new context. I like the screenplay now; I think I've done a good job with it. It took nine months and I'm still working on it. But I learned a lot from that work. In many ways it's better than the book, swifter, more unified and cohesive, fairer.

Question: When the producer says that, it sounds marvelous. Another question: Will you be shooting in color?

Kazan: I've always had a belief that color can be handled but

I'm not sure I'm right. I've worked in color several times and have always been very careful to talk things out with the cameraman. In the color films I've done, I've liked parts of them very much, others not. I thought the end of *East of Eden* was beautiful, and I thought the outdoor stuff in *Wild River,* especially at the end, was beautiful. And I thought that some of *Splendor in the Grass* was excellent. But the best camera work I think I've ever had was the black-and-white work that Boris Kaufman did in *Baby Doll* and *On the Waterfront.* Both of those films are photographically so subtle and so poetic.

Question: I think the love scene in *On the Waterfront* is one of the most poetic love scenes I've ever seen.

Kazan: I do believe, however, that one of the problems with color is that it was invented and set up labwise to be candy. The color itself was a form of entertainment, a novelty. "Look how colorful this is! Look how pretty and juicy this is!" The color that we use in films and the labs and the stock itself were devised, not haphazardly or accidentally, but quite consciously and scientifically to be as "colorful" and un-lifelike as possible. All of us have fought against it, have said, "Well, we're going to underexpose and force in the lab. We're going to double-print with a gray negative added." And so on. We've done all kinds of things to deal with this problem, always with the hope of getting color that is an emphasis factor, the way color is in life, and to catch the poetry of the essential gray in life.

Question: Which film-makers do you admire today, and why?

Kazan: I admire the film-makers I admire for the same reason I admire other artists—not essentially because their techniques are new or their techniques are like the ones I happen to have used, but because of the degree of humanity, the amount of human feeling they have. For example, one of the film-makers I admire most is a very conventional stylist, but a most unusual man. His name is Jean Renoir, and he is one of the great film-makers of the world. I always see Hitchcock's films and they always entertain me, but I don't think there's much in them. The films of Jean Renoir seem clumsier but they enlist me, and finally I have an experience with them. The same with Ray, some of his films are so slow and seem almost pointless. But by the time you are through with them, you have lived through something with their maker. Of the American film-makers I like John Ford in his prime. I think some of the younger men are fine technicians, but today's new technique is tomorrow's TV cliché. Whether there's jump-cutting or not, whether the screen is full of six images or sixty, I don't think means a damn thing. It's what's done with it. John Ford had soul.

Question: People say that films are an art form, but don't have any great ability to change society or a way of living. How do you feel about that?

Kazan: Any good art changes the way life is being lived but not in a mechanical, directly visible way. Certainly the great Russian films of the twenties when the spirit of that revolution was being celebrated must have made people feel that their lives had been worth living and the sacrifices they were making were worth making. I think some of our films of the forties and fifties changed human life in the sense that they deepened people's feeling of compassion for each other and their understanding of each other. That is what a great poet, whether he works in prose, in poetry, in paint or in stone, in images, or in the theater does. He makes you feel the humanity of other people. And of yourself—often to your surprise. That's no small achievement. It makes you able to live with people better, with more understanding, with more of what's called tolerance and with more joy too.

Question: Do you think that because we've been bombarded with so many images that film—although it's very much in vogue now as art form—will lose its effectiveness just because we have too much going on around us?

Kazan: Nonsense! People also say the novel is dying! Nonsense! I look forward to reading quite a few books. Things go up and then things come down, and then back up again. It has very little to do with whether the form is worn out. When someone has something to say, a passion about life, when that feeling inhabits any form, it's worth listening to. Music. "Christ," you say, "who wants to hear the same old symphonies?" It depends who wrote them.

Question: Talking about music, when you prepare the night before do you have—some people do have—a musical pattern in mind, a rhythmic cutting pattern?

Kazan: No. Naturally I try to have some idea about the first shot. But the thing I try to get hold of most securely is what the essential moment, the climax of the scene I'm to do that day, is and how it should look. If I can, I try to find some way in my mind of expressing that climax so that it is as exact and as revealing as I can make it. I say, "Well, what's the essence of that scene? The high point? How am I going to convey that?" Then I'll know what I am building toward. If I know where I'm going, I can get there. That's the thing I try to work out the night before. I think about it when I'm lying in bed in the morning. I try to think, "Now, what's the instant that tells everything about that scene?" It may be nothing more than a look on someone's face. But it will be the goal I'm aiming for that day.

Question: Let me ask you a specific question about one scene, the scene in *Viva Zapata!* in the church. When I felt the love so strongly between the couple, was this something that just happened, or that you thought about ahead of time?

Kazan: The main thing I thought of was—well, that love scene would play, Brando would do it well, and Jean would too—Jean Peters—but the thing I thought of that brought the scene to life was the fact that Zapata's brother was there in the church. The sense of danger, and poignancy, was due to his anxious presence in that scene. And when I thought of that, I had the scene.

Question: What about the scene in the cab in *On the Waterfront*?

Kazan: That scene was Brando's doing. I don't think I contributed much. The really touching thing was something Brando put in—he just said, "Oh, Charlie," in a certain way. Remember? I don't think he knew he was going to do it or how, but he was so much in the scene it just came out. The tone of his voice at that instant was what made that scene. And what was on his face, that made it. No director could have told an actor to do that. At his best, Brando was the best actor we've had in this country in my time. There's been no one like him. I mean, I get a lot of credit for that scene, but I don't deserve it. All I did was put the camera on the two fellows, and they're both good actors, Steiger too, but Brando had this very special genius in those days.

Question: It seems that Marlon Brando has never done work as good as the work he did with you.

Kazan: Well, he did trust me and that makes a difference. We understood each other and—well, he was very trusting of me, and therefore relaxed, not on guard, you know?

Question: This seems to be true when I think back on a great many performances. People like Lee Remick, whom I think is very talented, or Carroll Baker, whom I have never seen as good since *Baby Doll*. There seems to be a whole group of people. You must do something with your actors that somebody else doesn't do. And I would like to know what it is, if *you* know what it is.

Kazan: I don't know.

Question: Do you rehearse a lot? Do you spend a lot of time with them beforehand?

Kazan: Sometimes I do. I don't know. I talk to them . . .

Question: You mean you talk to them as people, not just as actors then?

Kazan: Any simplification is dangerous, but I guess I try to relate the moment of the scene they are about to play to something in their own lives so they understand it experientially, not only intellectually.

Question: Do you do the same kind of thing, for example, with people who haven't done films before? It's a pretty difficult thing to have them hit that mark on the stage floor and still have the emotion going.

Kazan: You can always make them hit the mark. That's not the problem. The problem is to make them not move mechanically. Sometimes you succeed in that and sometimes you don't.

Question: Well, what about working with professional actors versus the non-actors you used so much in your *Face in the Crowd*?

Kazan: Non-actors are awfully willing, you know. If you show some confidence in them, they're thrilled. So you just get them going, laugh and kid with them, become one of them, and before you know it they've forgotten all about the camera. Also you minimize the mechanics. You don't say, "You have to hit this mark." You put a table there or a chair or a stick on the floor so they can't go any farther. And so on. As a matter of fact you don't do differently with professionals.

Question: Do you think that the creative artist tends toward the liberal in politics? Or should?

Kazan: I should think so, yes. They're generally full of hopes for man's improving himself; they wish something for man. If they're artists, they have a vision larger than the immediate, and they have a purpose which is unarticulated often, but it's a human purpose, and not a profit purpose. I don't like businessmen in the arts much. I get along with them, I suppose, because I have to. But the whole thing about art is that it's much greater than any business and much greater than anything. It's the highest religion because it deals only with man's spirit, and when you deal with that, you're dealing with what's holy. Sometimes you see a home movie, an amateur film, a student film, a documentary, a newsreel, and you see an instant of sudden light, insight, the fellow who held the camera on his shoulder photographed something that no one else saw or could have seen, only *he* could have put it on the film. That's beautiful—when it's unique and personal and unexpected.

Question: Don't you also think part of it is what the audience brings to the theaters? You have to have enough people that bring something of themselves in to watch whatever you are putting up there?

Kazan: Well, yes, God bless 'em, they're getting more numerous, they're getting quicker, and they love films. I went to that *2001*——

Question: How did you like it?

Kazan: I liked it. It had some kind of poetry. I admire the man for making it. Anyway, that big barn of a Century Theatre was full of young people, and they were so intrigued with *2001,* so enlisted, that you felt it was *their* film. If an artist gives you something that speaks for you as well as *to* you—expresses what you feel that you can't express yourself—well, you should be very grateful to him.

Question: What about the fact that we still don't have any government subsidy for film-makers. How would you feel about government subsidy?

Kazan: I think there should be all kinds of subsidies. That doesn't mean that all films or all theater productions should be subsidized. There's a danger I've always felt that an outfit like George Stevens, Jr.'s outfit, the government agency that put up the funds for the American Film Institute—well, I was speaking to Stevens the other day and he said, "I watch over the film institute people so they don't get too starchy." The thing is you have to allow things, even encourage things you don't like yourself, because if they're someone's true feeling, well, let's help them speak out!

Question: What do you think about the so-called revolution in thinking and morals that's going on?

Kazan: About time! I mean, I'm all for it. I think our morals are worn out, mostly hypocritical and rarely given more than lip-service. I think marriage—I said it in my book—marriage is in so many cases hypocritical, and——

Question: It's almost an economic institution, isn't it?

Kazan: There's a growing gap between the way people live and the way they pretend to live. There's a profound and swelling hypocrisy in our society, and that's now being shown up by young people. They're saying, "Let's talk about the way it really is, let's talk about facts, and not the way you want to pretend to each other that you live." And the whole middle-class set of values is being re-scrutinized, and they ask, "Is that way of living or pretending to live really worth anything? You guys have mucked up the world, and hundreds of kids a week are being killed in Vietnam. For what? For this? The hell with it! We won't go."

Question: Do you think that's the evidence of theater, too, with things like *Hair,* for example, and . . .

Kazan: I like *Hair,* but I think it's going to be much better than that in time and very soon, too. I think the new ones in the theater are going to be speaking very seriously. I think *Hair* is good and fresh and sometimes beautiful, but there's better and tougher coming.

Question: Which brings me around to another question: What about censorship of any kind?

Kazan: I'm against censorship of any kind. I think everything should be thrown into the light and let people see what they want to see. But there is one contradiction in my feelings. I always feel nervous when I see young children watching sadism on the screen. I wish it weren't there. I wish they weren't watching it because there *is* something beguiling about it. Everyone's full of antagonisms, and there is something beguiling about Jimmy Cagney, say, punching somebody, and so maybe children are thinking, "Well, it's fun. I'd like to push a grapefruit in someone's face." But still, I feel censorship is wrong. One thing I like about what John Lindsay is doing here in the city now is that we have these dirty movies. Not many people go to them, mostly old codgers that don't get a charge out of life any other way. But they're there, so no one can say, "They won't let us show this or that or the other." What the hell? I mean, you have movies that show the sex act. So what? But they're not censored and that fact alone, I think, is important.

Question: What about the stuff they see on television? You know, Vietnam? I mean, this seems to some people almost the worst kind of immorality.

Kazan: I think the news programs on television are tremendous. The coverage of the war in Vietnam has been one of the things that has caused the great feeling against the war. When you see our best fellows being killed and maimed and carried away, when you see the Vietnamese people, south and north, too, but particularly who the enemy is, the North Vietnamese, slim beautiful young men and women, killed, captured, terrified, you must say, "This is wrong, what the hell, I don't want to be their terrifier. I don't want to be their killer. I don't want to be their capturer." That's basic. Beyond any politics. Everybody who's seen those scenes on TV must feel that. That's why I think the whole TV coverage is one of the best things that has been happening.

Question: Well, one last question, about critics. Do critics influence you or bother you? Let's take theater, films, and the book?

Kazan: Sometimes I've gotten stimulus from critics. They've said things I've valued. A lot of the criticism about me as co-director of the Lincoln Center Repertory Company was valid. I didn't enjoy it when it was being shot at me, but the fact is I wasn't suited to that job, and I finally thought the fellows who said that were accurate. Their hostile criticism of me made me reexamine myself and my work there and say to myself, "You honestly don't want to do that."

The great thing criticism can do is illuminate. There's one great theater critic in this country, his name's Harold Clurman, and every time I read one of his articles, I see more in the plays than I would have otherwise. After you've read good criticism, you see more. It enriches your experience, and I think there's a great function. I'm not against it by any means.

Of course, there are guys who are trying to get up quick by knocking down everybody.

Question: But don't you think sometimes, in your case, they have been criticizing you and not necessarily the piece of work?

Kazan: I'd say when you criticize a man's work, you are certainly criticizing him. And vice versa. And why not?

PLAYWRIGHTS

Table-Talk of G.B.S.: The Drama, the Theatre, and the Films
by ARCHIBALD HENDERSON

The dining-room at 10 Adelphi Terrace, London. Time: late March, 1924, just after the production of Shaw's latest play, "Saint Joan," at the New Theatre, London. A room full of sunshine over-looking the narrow gorge of the Adelphi. The walls are sparsely dec-orated, the principal object in the room (besides the original) being a portrait of Bernard Shaw which startlingly confronts you on en-tering the room—the impressionist, poster-like portrait by Augustus John, with flying locks and moustaches, rectangular head, and ex-aggeratedly flouting lower lip—done in bright colours: reds, yel-lows, blues. Its close analogue, a superior study and a better likeness, hangs in the Fitzwilliam Museum at Cambridge. Bernard Shaw and Archibald Henderson discovered seated at opposite ends of the dinner-table, à deux. During the course of the meal the food is often sadly neglected for the sake of argument—the Irishman waving his long arms and tapering fingers, the American energetically ham-mering his closed right fist in his left, open palm.

Henderson: Well, I must say you made a neat get-away at the New the other night. One moment I was talking to you in your private box and the next Miss Sybil Thorndike was explaining to

From Table-Talk of G.B.S., *by Archibald Henderson, pp. 53–65.* *Copyright © 1925 by George Bernard Shaw and Archibald Henderson;* *renewed 1953 by Archibald Henderson. Reprinted by permission of* *Harper & Row, Publishers, Inc.*

an audience stentoriously shouting "Author! Author!" that, *as usual under such circumstances,* the author was not to be found. Your wife and Miss Lena Ashwell must have spirited you mysteriously away. I felt defrauded—robbed of a long-anticipated pleasure of hearing you make a footlight speech. Of course, I understood that you wished Miss Thorndike to have all the honours for playing beautifully the title role in your greatest play.

And now to come to the films. Has the enormous development of the cinema industry benefited the drama, or the reverse?

Shaw: No: the huge polynational audience makes mediocrity compulsory. Films must aim at the average of an American millionaire and a Chinese coolie, a cathedral-town governess and a mining-village barmaid, because they have to go everywhere and please everybody. They spread the drama enormously; but as they must interest a hundred per cent. of the population of the globe, barring infants in arms, they cannot afford to meddle with the upper-ten-per-cent. theatre of the highbrows or the lower-ten-per-cent. theatre of the blackguards. The result is that the movie play has supplanted the old-fashioned tract and Sunday School prize: it is reeking with morality but dares not touch virtue. And virtue, which is defiant and contemptuous of morality even when it has no practical quarrel with it, is the life-blood of high drama.

Henderson: In spite of the fame of certain artistic directors—the Griffiths, De Milles, Lubitschs, and Dwans—perhaps it is true that the film industry is, for the most part, directed and controlled by people with imperfectly developed artistic instincts and ideals who have their eyes fixed primarily on financial rewards.

Shaw: All industries are brought under the control of such people by Capitalism. If the capitalists let themselves be seduced from their pursuit of profits to the enchantments of art, they would be bankrupt before they knew where they were. You cannot combine the pursuit of money with the pursuit of art.

Henderson: Would it not be better for film magnates to engage first-rate authors to write directly for the films, paying them handsomely for their work, rather than pay enormous prices to an author of novel, story, or play, and then engage a hack at an absurdly low price to prepare a scenario?

Shaw: Certainly not first-rate authors: democracy always prefers second-bests. The magnates might pay for literate subtitles; but one of the joys of the cinema would be gone without such gems as "Christian: Allah didst make thee wondrous strong and fair." Seriously, though, the ignorance which leads to the employment of uneducated people to do professional work in modern industry is a scandal. It is just as bad in journalism. In my youth all writing was done by men who, if they had little Latin and less Greek, had at any rate been in schools where there was a pretence of teaching them; and they had all read the Bible, however reluctantly. Nowadays that has all gone: literary work is entrusted to men and women so illiterate that the mystery is how they ever learned their alphabet. They know next to nothing else, apparently. I agree with you as to the scenarios founded on existing plays and novels. Movie plays should be invented expressly for the screen by original imaginative visualizers. But you must remember that just as all our music consists of permutations and combinations of twelve notes, all our fiction consists of variations on a few plots; and it is in the words that the widest power of variation lies. Take that away and you will soon be so hard up for a new variation that you will snatch at anything—even at a Dickens plot—to enable you to carry on.

Henderson: American newspapers and magazines teem with articles, interviews, counsels, and admonitions regarding the films and measures for their improvement. Have you in mind any definite suggestions for the further artistic development of films?

Shaw (explosively): Write better films, if you can: there is no other way. Development must come from the centre, not from the periphery. The limits of external encouragement have been reached long ago. Take a highbrow play to a Little Theatre and ask the management to spend two or three thousand dollars on the production, and they will tell you that they cannot afford it. Take an opium eater's dream to Los Angeles and they will realize it for you: the more it costs the more they will believe in it. You can have a real Polar expedition, a real volcano, a reconstruction of the Roman Forum on the spot: anything you please, provided it is enormously costly. Wasted money, mostly. If the United States Government put a limit of twenty-five thousand dollars to the expenditure on any single non-educational film, the result would probably be an enormous improvement in the interest of the film drama, because film magnates would be forced to rely on dramatic imagination instead of on mere spectacle. Oh, those scenes of oriental voluptuousness as imagined by a whaler's cabin boy! They would make a monk of Don Juan. Can you do nothing to stop them?

Henderson: The only way to stop them is with ridicule. That is why I am making you talk. Already such scenes are greeted with ribald laughter and shouts of unholy glee in many American communities. But our happiest effects are achieved by having English duchesses impersonated by former cloak models, Italian counts by former restaurant waiters. In spite of all this the triumph of the American film is spectacular. The invasion of England and Europe is a smashing success. London, Paris, Berlin are placarded with announcements of American films: they are literally everywhere. "The Covered Wagon," "Scaramouche," "The Hunchback of Notre Dame," "The Ten Commandments," "Mother," "Nanook": Mary Pickford, Douglas Fairbanks, Charlie Chaplin, Jackie Coogan, etc., etc. Yet I am told that the Italians make the best films; and the best European picture I saw in Europe was a Swedish film at the Gaumont "Picture Palace" in Paris. The triumph, almost the monopoly of the American film is uncontested. But are American films superior to all others?

Shaw (decisively): No. Many of them are full of the stupidest errors of judgment. Overdone and foolishly repeated strokes of expression, hideous make-ups, close-ups that an angel's face would not bear, hundreds of thousands of dollars spent on spoiling effects that I or any competent producer could secure quickly and certainly at a cost of ten cents, featureless over-exposed faces against underexposed backgrounds, vulgar and silly subtitles, impertinent lists of everybody employed in the film from the star actress to the press agent's office boy: these are only a few of the *gaffes* American film factories are privileged to make. Conceit is rampant among your film makers; and good sense is about non-existent. That is where Mr. Chaplin scores; but Mr. Harold Lloyd seems so far to be the only rival intelligent enough to follow his example. We shall soon have to sit for ten minutes at the beginning of every reel to be told who developed it, who fixed it, who dried it, who provided the celluloid, who sold the chemicals, and who cut the author's hair. Your film people simply don't know how to behave themselves: they take liberties with the public at every step on the strength of their reckless enterprise and expenditure. Every American aspirant to film work should be sent to Denmark or Sweden for five years to civilize him before being allowed to enter a Los Angeles studio.

Henderson: Well! that's that! And how surprised and pained some American producers will be to read your cruel words! But too much success is not good for anyone—not even for you. And speaking of comets, can plays of conversation—"dialectic dramas"—like yours be successfully filmed?

Shaw: Barrie says that the film play of the future will have no pictures and will consist exclusively of sub-titles.

Henderson: I wonder if conversation dramas are not on the wane—since the public in countless numbers patronizes, revels in the silent drama.

Shaw: If you come to that, the public in overwhelming numbers is perfectly satisfied with no drama at all. But the silent drama is producing such a glut of spectacle that people are actually listening to invisible plays by wireless. The silent drama is exhausting the resources of silence. Charlie Chaplin and his very clever colleague Edna Purviance, Bill Hart and Alla Nazimova, Douglas Fairbanks and Mary Pickford, Harold Lloyd and Buster Keaton, have done everything that can be done in dramatic dumb show and athletic stunting, and played all the possible variations on it. The man who will play them off the screen will not be their superior at their own game but an Oscar Wilde of the movies who will flash epigram after epigram at the spectators and thus realize Barrie's anticipation of more subtitles than pictures.

Henderson: If that is true, then why—since wit and epigram are your familiar weapons—why have none of your plays been filmed?

Shaw (*deadly resolute*): Because I wouldn't let them. I repeat that a play with the words left out is a play spoiled; and all those filmings of plays written to be spoken as well as seen are boresome blunders except when the dialogue is so worthless that it is a hindrance instead of a help. Of course that is a very large exception in point of bulk; but the moment you come to classic drama, the omission of the words and the presentation of the mere scenario is very much as if you offered as a statue the wire skeleton which supports a sculptor's modelling clay. Besides, consider the reaction on the box office. People see a Macbeth film. They imagine they have seen "Macbeth," and don't want to see it again; so when your Mr. Hackett or somebody comes round to act the play, he finds the house empty. That is what has happened to dozens of good plays whose authors have allowed them to be filmed. It shall not happen to mine if I can help it.

Interview with Harold Pinter
and Clive Donner
by KENNETH CAVANDER

Harold Pinter's play, The Caretaker, *gave him his widest audience. It became his first film. Produced without guarantee of distribution, financed by private subscription, and shot entirely on location at the top of an old house in Hackney, the film involved Pinter and his director, Clive Donner, in an exceptionally close and successful collaboration. Donner, then editor of* Genevieve *and director of several major films, worked with Pinter from the beginning on the script. When they had reached the final stages of editing, I went to visit them to find out their reactions to what had been, for both of them, a new experience.*

Interviewer: What experiences did you have with the film industry before *The Caretaker* film?

Pinter: Well, I'd written an adaptation of a novel. Before I went into *The Caretaker* I'd only done that. I'd never been in a film studio except once as an extra.

Interviewer: How did the idea of making *The Caretaker* start?

Pinter: Donald Pleasance had a great deal to do with it. But we all had it in mind, and then Donald, Bob Shaw and myself discussed it, and finally Donald got on to Clive about it.

Donner: Yes, Donald asked me whether I thought a film of *The Caretaker* could be made, and how, and what it would cost. I said I thought a film could be made with a very economical budget, shooting on location, with very little adaptation, very little expansion of the play. As far as the budget was concerned, I said we could make it for £40,000. In fact it cost £30,000.

Interviewer: Does that mean that in effect the initiative came from the actors and yourself?

Donner: Yes, in a sense.

Interviewer: And then what happened?

Donner: We met Harold for luncheon one day. . . .

Pinter: I paid for the lunch.

Donner: He paid for the lunch. We said, "We think a film could be made of this."

Pinter: I was very suspicious.

Donner: He was very suspicious.

Interviewer: Had you been approached to make adaptations of your own work before?

Pinter: Yes, but I'd never agreed to anything.

Interviewer: Why?

Pinter: The circumstances didn't seem right. I thought there were all sorts of things needed for film production which I wasn't prepared to deal with. And I was extremely reluctant to make a film of *The Caretaker* because I thought I couldn't possibly get anything fresh from the subject. I'd been associated with the play, you see, through various productions in London and New York for a couple of years.

Interviewer: What persuaded you this time?

Pinter: It might have been something about . . . I don't know, the general common sense and relaxation of the people I met. I put up a lot of defense mechanisms about it, and said I couldn't possibly even write the draft of a screenplay, couldn't do anything at all, and then someone said, "You don't have to do anything" (though it turned out I did) . . . and I let myself be won over. I was behaving rather like a child about it.

Donner: I think it's slightly unfair to say that you've been behaving like a child. I think you were expecting a more conventional approach to the adaptation of the work.

Interviewer: How did you get over this feeling of having worked through it?

Pinter: Well, I suppose it was because no one said to me, "This is a film with a capital F." That would have frightened me off, I think. They simply said, "This is the idea, this is the work, these are the characters—how can it all be transposed into a film in keeping with what we have, what must be there." We had long discussions about it and I worked out a kind of draft.

Interviewer: [to Donner] Did you feel you were making the script from the beginning? Do you know what I mean?

Donner: Not quite, no.

Interviewer: Well, I suppose ideally one thinks of the director as working from the beginning, on the conception, and then through to the final screenplay. Ideally. Agreed?

Donner: Well yes, but it very rarely happens. It's certainly not happened to me. Yet.

Interviewer: And here you're faced with a script that is settled—not only settled but has been running for a long time. A *fait accompli.*

Donner: Oh no, I don't think that's quite true.

Interviewer: In what ways wasn't it true?

Pinter: Well, Clive and I did work intensively on the script when I really got excited about the idea. We saw it as a film, and we worked on it as a film. We weren't thinking about something that was set in any kind of pattern. There was an obvious overall pattern to the work, but we had to see it and work on it in terms of movement from one thing to another.

Donner: And you see there's a sort of compulsion in film makers to "open out" (whatever that means) subjects that they set out to film. I decided from the beginning that this approach was a blind alley. It seemed to me that within the situation, and within the relationships that developed between the characters, there was enough action, enough excitement seen through the eye of a film camera, without imposing conventional film action treatment.

Pinter: It seemed to me that when you have two people standing on the stairs and one asks the other if he would like to be caretaker in this house, and the other bloke, you know, who is work-shy, doesn't want in fact to say no, he doesn't want the job, but at the same time he wants to edge it around. . . . Now it seems to me there's an enormous amount of internal conflict within one of the characters and external conflict between them—and it's exciting cinema.

Donner: The fact that it doesn't cover enormous landscapes and there aren't hordes of horses galloping in one direction and hordes of bison in the other has nothing to do with it. It's a different sort of action, but it's still action. And it's still capable of being encompassed in the cinema.

Pinter: You can say the play has been "opened out" in the sense that things I'd yearned to do, without knowing it, in writing for the stage, crystallized when I came to think about it as a film. Until then I didn't know that I wanted to do them because I'd accepted the limitations of the stage. For instance, there's a scene in the garden of the house, which is very silent; two silent figures with a third looking on. I think in the film one has been able to hit the relationship of the brothers more clearly than in the play.

Donner: What I think Harold means when he says that the film has developed on what happened for him in the theater, with particular reference to the relationship between the brothers, is that the psychological richness of the original play was to a certain extent hampered by the need to project out into a theater.

Pinter: Yes, I think the actors on the stage are under the delusion that they have to project in a particular way. There's a scene in the film, also in the play, when the elder brother asks the other if he'd like to be caretaker in the place. On film it's played in terms of great intimacy and I think it's extraordinarily successful. They speak quite normally, it's a quiet scene, and it works. But on stage it didn't ever work like that. The actors get a certain kind of comfort, I think, in the fact that they're so close to the camera.

Donner: The cinema obviously can deal with that very much more subtly and specifically. I think that the writing is such that

The Caretaker isn't just a piece of theater, but it can go further and further and discover more and more facts to the characters, so that rather than repeating what happened in the theater one can enrich and develop it much more surely.

Pinter: I'm not sure I agree that the cinema will be able to gain in subtlety. I think that when one talks in these terms one thinks of a stage miles away with a vast audience and the characters very small. But I think you can be as subtle on a stage as you can in the film. You just do it in a different way. In this case the director understood what was necessary and what I, the fellow who had written it, meant. Which is a very rare thing. I'd always understood that everything is always bastardized in films, and that film people were a real lot of fakes, phonies, charlatans. The whole relationship between the people concerned was something I hadn't quite met in any medium.

Interviewer: So you had the script. Did you ever consider going through the normal production-distribution channels to make the film?

Pinter: Yes, in fact we not only considered it, we were involved in it. We were right up to our necks in a very affable relationship with an American international distribution organization, but at the last moment they pulled out.

Donner: We'd also had a great deal of interest from certain sources in England, but in the end they all got slightly cold feet—very cold feet. Then this American distributor pulled out, leaving us committed to crew, house, and various other expenditures.

Interviewer: And that's the point where you collected the money by subscription?

Donner: Well, we either had to dip into our pockets and pay everybody off, and not make the film, or we had to decide to go on and make the film. Peter Hall, who'd been involved in the financial support of the stage production, had said early on, "If you'd like some support from me on this I'd be happy to give it." When this particular crisis occurred we took him up on that and realized there was a possibility of raising the rest of the money, in the same way.

Interviewer: Do you find that exhilarating as a way of doing things—or suspenseful—or just hell?

Pinter: My feelings were clear. I hated the whole dealing with the

American company from the start. I distrusted it, and I was right to distrust it. They proved eminently untrustworthy, and good luck! I think part of their—excuse me, what am I saying? They *must* be untrustworthy, otherwise they would cease to be respected. . . . So we all sat down in a pub, and we had a marvelous name-dropping session of everyone we were going to write to, all the people who sympathized either with us personally or with the play. We wrote to them, we expressed terms in the letter, and we were oversubscribed. We turned away £60,000. We really thrust through, and what was suddenly clear about it was that each and every one of us wanted to do the film. It was a great moment, that. I had been full of disgust and nausea and spleen and whiskey, and we could so easily have said, "To hell with the whole thing. What's the point?" I could have certainly. It was confirming my darkest suspicion about the film industry. But we didn't. . . .

Donner: And it wasn't only Harold. It was Mike Birkett, and Donald Pleasance and . . .

Pinter: Not only that. If we're going to indulge in a bit of remembrance—I remember so well that the continuity girl who was down there at the time, engaged by our company, such as it was, a very rocky company, she suddenly, sitting in this pub, offered to put in some money.

Interviewer: How long did it take to collect the total?

Pinter: I think from the time we decided, it was about a fortnight.

Interviewer: So then you were ready to go.

Donner: Well, during this period we were in fact already rehearsing, and we spent two, three days of our rehearsal time sitting around scratching our heads. So that although we went forward with a certain amount of renewed confidence once we'd decided on the thing, each time that Michael Birkett came upstairs into the room where we were rehearsing with another telephone message, another telegram saying that Noel Coward or somebody or other had come forward, it was very exciting . . . and frequently stimulating.

Interviewer: But you got it all before you started shooting?

Pinter: Yes, we had assured promises of all the money before we started shooting.

Interviewer: Apart from this crisis while you were rehearsing, the thing went more or less as scheduled?

Pinter: Yes, except we lost a few days sitting around eating salt beef sandwiches.

Donner: If anybody had come forward then, and offered the amount of money that would have made it possible for us to shoot the film in a studio, or in a more lavish way, I wouldn't have taken it.

Interviewer: Did you ever think you might do it in a studio?

Donner: No, never!

Pinter: I wish the actors were here to ask, but I'm sure that for them it was tremendous—I'm sorry to say this, it sounds rather strange, almost as if I'm asking for realism, which I'm not—but I think it did an awful lot for the actors to go up real stairs, open real doors in a house which existed, with a dirty garden and a back wall.

Interviewer: You were there every minute of the shooting?

Pinter: Not entirely. I arrived late quite often.

Donner: I think Harold was there most of the time.

Pinter: I don't know whether other script writers are there to the extent I was.

Interviewer: How did you react to it?

Pinter: As a complete layman to the film medium I found that looking around that room where one had to crouch to see what was going on (the whole film was shot in a kneeling or crouching posture)—I found there was a smell to it. Since then I've been down to a studio, Shepperton, and things are very different. You don't have to crouch, you don't have to kneel, you can absolutely stand up straight, there are lots of lights, the walls open, they float, that's the word, float, and you've got no worries at all. Well, I found the limitations on location, in this house, gave a freshness to the work. I think the actors found that too. They found new answers, answers they hadn't been able to find or at least hadn't within the circumstances been able to find when they were playing it on the stage.

Donner: And on location, like this house, I find one is dealing in tones of gray. There are no blacks and whites. The sets, the photography, are seen in terms of gray rather than in terms of black. . . .

Pinter: What I'm very pleased about myself is that in the film, as opposed to the play, we see a real house and real snow outside, dirty snow, and the streets. We don't see them very often but they're there, the backs of houses and windows, attics in the distance. There is actually sky as well, a dirty one, and these characters move in the context of a real world—as I believe they do. In the play, when people were confronted with just a set, a room and a door, they often assumed it was all taking place in limbo, in a vacuum, and the world outside hardly existed, or had existed at some point but was only half-remembered. Now one thing which I think is triumphantly expressed in the film is Clive's concentration on the characters when they are outside the room, outside the house. Not that there aren't others. There are others. There are streets, there is traffic, shadows, shapes about, but he is for me concentrating on the characters as they walk, and while we go into the world outside it is almost as if only these characters exist.

Interviewer: What struck me just now was your thoroughness in following the film through the editing stages.

Pinter: Well, this editing stage was for me, of course, completely new. It was the first time, and an absolute eye opener.

Interviewer: I can see you were enjoying it.

Pinter: It's great. It's great that one can move from one thing to another, or duplicate it, or cut it out, the wreck that can be wreaked in editing.

Donner: Havoc, you mean?

Pinter: The havoc, yes, the havoc is terrifying.

Interviewer: But you must have been involved in television productions, and to that extent you must have had some feeling for what happened and what you could do. You know what pictures roughly you're going to use, in about the same way as you know in a film.

Pinter: But it's very primitive. All that's open to you is just a position of sequences, or possibly cuts, but you haven't got the flexibility that you have in films. For instance in this particular play, there was a moment on stage when the two brothers smiled at each other. That was it. One stood on one side of the stage and the other stood on the other, and they smiled briefly.

Interviewer: That was written into the text?

Pinter: Oh yes. And then one of them exited and that was that. Now, on film, either you're going to hold both things, in other words, the two brothers smiling, then one goes out. But it isn't the same as the stage, you don't get the complex thing which makes it so much of a moment on the stage. The distance, the separation cannot be the same. The balance, the timing, and the rhythm to this, the silent music, as it were, are determined in so many different ways, and I know we both felt, Clive and I, there was something to come there. I said something, I don't know what, and Clive said, "We want to go from one to the other, one to the other. Now the balance of the whole thing is that if you don't go to the other then there's no point made, but if you go from the other back to the first then the point is over-made. The balance, the editing balance, is crucial, as everyone knows, but it needs an eye and a relaxation which the film affords you, and no other medium can. You can sift it, you see, and the sifting is of value. Of course, on the stage, you can say to the girl, "Go out, this won't do, try another one. . . ." And if you make a decision and you're proved wrong, you correct it. But in films you're dealing with something that's going to be finished once you make a decision. You cannot go on changing ad infinitum, and you may make a decision and six months later you say, "That was entirely wrong."

Donner: This is very interesting about such a moment as the smile. To a certain extent, in the theater, one entrusts the satisfactory presentation of this moment entirely to the actors. You expect that they have either consciously or intuitively sensed the way an audience is going with them and the play at a particular moment, and they can adjust their performance each night, to each audience. Now one of the things that actors feel terribly strongly about in the cinema is that their performances are taken out of their hands. They resent this, and I understand it completely. It seems to me a miserable thing to have to accept, particularly with the sort of actors we have in this film, who are extremely intelligent men, extremely successful, extremely creative. They do it, then they go away to other films, other projects, and leave us with the film to edit in a way that ultimately we have to take a decision alone. Well, as Harold says, you may decide at this moment that one thing is right, and six months later you see it, and you say, "I was wrong"—and actors, alas, have to accept this.

Pinter: Surely with this film, all the actors would subscribe to what is being done. Because we weren't asking them merely to go on there and give their performances as such; we were asking to examine how you should give your performance in relation to producing a finished film.

Donner: To take creative responsibility, which is the aim of all these ventures, I think.

Interviewer: So now the thing's done. Do you know how, or when, it will come out?

Pinter: Well, not precisely, no. It'll be shown, that's all I know at the moment.

Donner: There's not much we can say about this, except that I think this piece is not solely an art house film, or need not be.

Interviewer: In other words, you don't want it to be.

Donner: Well, I don't think it need be, because from my own experience of seeing audiences react to the play, both in London and New York, I know that much wider audiences than would be reached by an art house release, enjoyed the play. But at the same time I think it would be very wrong to put this film out on ordinary general release—for two reasons. One, because I think the piece, by its nature, demands a concentration, a special attention which even unsophisticated audiences coming in coach tours to the Duchess Theatre in London brought with them—by virtue of the fact that they'd made a special journey to be there. Now, I don't think that people going out to their local cinema will make that same special effort, and I think the piece does require an effort for an audience to appreciate, to be able to enjoy it. And I think the other reason why I would not like a general release is because I think it would be very bad if, after all the hoo-ha of a full general release, it failed. Not only for its own sake, but because I think it would then tend to muck up the chances of another film that we or anybody else might make, and which might demand less of its audience than this. I think somewhere between a full general release and limited art house release there is a market for *The Caretaker* which I would like to find.

Interviewer: So what you're trying to do is trace this special audience.

Donner: Well, I would just like to have it exposed to a wider audience than an art house audience, but not be lumbered with the full heavyweight responsibilities of exploitation costs and print costs which a full circuit release implies.

Interviewer: How do you expect to do this?

Donner: I think it can be done by cinemas agreeing to show it in certain locations where they know or suspect or are prepared to try and find out that there is an audience prepared to make the effort to come and see this film, and to enjoy it.

Interviewer: [to Pinter] Have you discussed any of this, or doesn't it interest you?

Pinter: Yes, it does interest me. But I think myself the work has been preserved in film, I think it's perfectly true to what I wrote, and I think it's funny. But really I simply feel that whatever happens with it, a lot of people are going to see it, and I can only come down again to the fact that what absolutely amazes me is that there it is. It's done and as far as I'm concerned it's absolutely on the nail.

Interviewer: So in a sense the kind of classification and squaring off that is done by the press and formers of public opinion no longer matters.

Pinter: Who cares? We all did it for nothing at all, no money, no conveniences, public conveniences, no facilities; the food was bloody awful, the curry was the same as the steak and kidney pudding, and I think it's been worth doing.

Theatre and Film:
The Misery of Comparison
by PETER HANDKE

Pascal said, approximately: all misery comes from man's constantly believing that he must compare himself with the infinite. And another misery—Pascal did not say this—comes from man's believing that he must, in general, compare.

As I write this, I see, outside in the street, two streetsweepers cleaning the sidewalk with huge brooms. Both have orange and white striped uniforms *like bicycle racers,* both have white, crumpled stockings *like tramps* or *like characters in a Beckett play,* both have faces *like Southerners,* both wear caps *like those in photographs of prisoners of war from the First World War,* both walk stiffed-kneed *like bums,* all three—now a third joins them, and a fourth—wear black mittens *like the snow removal crew in the winter,* all five are alike with their gigantic brooms and shovels, which make them appear quite small, *like figures in a painting by Breughel.*

But—one of the streetsweepers swept *faster than* the other, and the other streetsweeper wore his cap *lower* on his face *than* the one, and the other other streetsweeper had a much *more German* face *than* the other streetsweeper, and the other other other streetsweeper seemed to perform his work *more unwillingly than* the other other streetsweeper, and finally—meanwhile the men have moved from my view—the last streetsweeper came to mind because he had, it seemed, shoved the broom forward *more powerfully than* the others.

How do we arrive at this need to compare, at this search? (And I call it a search.) Does it not originate in the inability to distinguish individual things immediately? And how does it come about that we, while we compare, also want to evaluate every time at the same time? Is it not true that we evaluate because we are unable at first to perceive an object *dis*valued by the comparison? Because we, in short, look at it blindly; and from an utter helplessness, if we cannot perceive it thus, we slip immediately into comparison? The objects seem to be there only to be played off against each other. They become abstracted to possibilities for comparison: one avoids becoming clear about them by thoughtlessly measuring them against other objects. In this way a hierarchy of objects arises mechanically in the consciousness of the perceiver, which, like a customer, collects the objects. The first thought following perception is not a first thought, but on the contrary a reflex of comparison, as if we were buyers in a department store, presented not so much with a world of individual wares as with a world of possibilities for comparison. And I too have been able to help myself by nothing other than comparing: yes, comparisons help.

And the models for comparison to which all comparisons and devaluations may be reduced are the following: "I would rather have this than that," and "I would rather be this than that." And finally (of use for all objects, situations and incidents): "I like Negroes more than Chinamen," "I like the flatlands more than the mountains," "I like music more than painting," "I like democracy more than revolutions," "I like security more than insecurity," "I like my wife more than all movie stars put together," "I like the patriarch in Constantinople more than the Pope in Rome," "I like a strict order, in which everyone has his job and can eat until he is content more than a freedom in which . . ."—you can complete the sentences for yourself. It appears, then, that comparisons serve above all to talk away the compared object with a sentence. Any further preoccupation with it is unnecessary: it exists only as an object of comparison, as an object of value, as an object of feeling. The object transforms itself—it becomes an object of aversion. And the misery and the greatness of the art of comparison is that, with its help, every object becomes formalized in consciousness into an object of feeling and value. Every object in the world can come to be compared with every other object in the world. Everything is super- and sub-ordinated in the hierarchy of feeling—anything can be compared to anything else—nothing remains outside consciousness only because it is incomprehensible, strange, and complicated. Precisely because it is incomprehensible, strange, and complicated, no alternative remains but comparing. Comparison protects against preoccupation with the object. The incomprehensible object becomes an object of feeling; because it is incomprehensible other objects are preferable to it. For example, one's own skin, which one knows: everything is easily compared to one's own skin, and by the comparison is also in fact undeservingly trusted. The healthy perception celebrates its triumph—we can prove this later—in the great misery of comparison.

This seemingly long preface should only make us skeptical, and clarify the reaction mechanisms in a single, modest sentence. And it is the sentence whose model I wanted, tediously, to approach more and more closely. It is simply: "I like going to the movies more than to the theatre." (I would have liked to have been able to turn the sentence around, but it will be employed quite well in the following series.) What an expense about such a harmless sentence! "I like going to the movies more than to the theatre." I remember having already used the sentence myself repeatedly. I say "remember" because I have not used the sentence for some time. Does that mean that I now prefer going to the theatre? No, it means only that I no longer use the sentence, that I am embarrassed by using such a sentence. I still like going to the movies more. So, now I have used this sentence, but the more frequently I use it the more it bores me. It seems to me that as you can go through the same stream only once, so can you use the same sentence only once. The second time it is already a mistake; by the next time it is a disgrace; and finally it is only an idiocy. And as there is a wise saying of Kierkegaard's that one is not able to go through the same stream even once, so there is perhaps the wise saying that there are specific sentences that one cannot use even once without their being immediately mistakes, disgraces, and idiocies. And they are all those sentences whose models are conveyor-belt products of consciousness. Another is the sentence about theatre and the movies, which is understandable, perhaps, as a cry, like "Ow!" or "Aha!" or "Oh!" or "O God!" As *sentence,* however, it can no longer say anything to me—I can say it well enough, but I cannot hear it anymore.

Moreover, the sentence has also become something like a first and last cry. With it, everything is said about theatre and film, beginning and end. It is a model sentence, a modal sentence for young writers, young filmmakers—and even young dramatists—or whoever else we care to name. At present, the theater is in the position of having to defend itself. But what does *the* theatre mean? The theatre which the detractors of theatre mean is nothing but a ceremonial running at idle and gradually running out. The fights, which are decided in it in the form of dialogues, conflicts, stage laughter, trembling voices, burdensome silences, and actual fights, are—this is the paradox—in *reality apparent* fights, and the softest and most restrained chamber plays are as material nothing but flashy principal and state actions, principal and state reactions in the East and West. Enough of metaphors, enough of scolding, that is as boring as this theatre itself. A short time ago the students in Paris, with a circular and self-referring system of metaphor, cleared out and occupied the Théâtre Odéon. To be sure, the photos of it show that the quality of its playing space is still overwhelming, that the debaters in it are themselves romantic ornaments: so easily the talk about the old metaphors can become distorted. But, as I said, I have little desire to grind sentences long known to be true against this hurdy-gurdy theatre. Much more noteworthy, it seems to me, is the overdevelopment of films to the point in time where it is precisely the progressive films which are attentive to the great dilemma of film. That dilemma is that film, over a long period of time, simply by showing images and not by *describing* in the literary manner—simply by the abundant showing of images—has arrived gradually, with every new film, at an order of images that one can call a film syntax. A film image is no longer a pure *image;* it has become, through the history of all the film images before it, a "shot" or point of view. That means it shows the conscious or unconscious point of view of the filmmaker toward the filmed object, which in this way becomes the object of the filmmaker. Filmed, the object is abstracted by the shot, dematerialized —the shot of the object serves as the *expression* of the filmmaker. Because of the series of shots that have been produced which carry the same meaning, the shot turns into, one can say, a film sentence, which is built after the model of film sentences which already exist. The shot, the film sentence, now stands in already firmly canonized relationships to the preceding and succeeding shots and film sentences. The history of moving pictures, it is true, is more than the history of the formation of a standardized (and also standardizing) film syntax. In the beginning one could perhaps have asserted that a film did not need a description. Since then, however, film has had its own history, and the images of objects, the shots of objects, present themselves to the skillful film viewer as *descriptions* of the objects! That applies especially well to films which belong to particular genres and hold completely to the rules of those genres, as in crime movies, spy movies, westerns, horror movies, and so forth. Each image in these films is an image sentence which sticks to the syntax already established. I think of the shot in horror movies in which a person is seen walking up to the camera, and as the face grows larger you become more frightened, and suddenly an inch in front of the camera, something horrible happens to the person, and in the action is the rule (I say: the rule!) that the huge contorted face must now open its eyes wide and scream chillingly, or in any case try to scream—at which point a hand, perhaps a gloved hand, instantly spreads over the face. The shot, of course, has another meaning if, some meters in front of the camera, the person turns to the left or right and disappears from view: this image sentence quiets us—nothing will happen to the person. The fright that we have in genre films when a person is shown from the rear, I do not need to recall in detail, nor the anxiety that we feel for the hero of westerns when he is shown riding along a rock ledge and the edge of the cliff above is still empty. I would mention, however, a flowery phrase of the film grammar introduced into the film language by Alfred Hitchcock. He not only shows close-ups of beautiful women such as

Grace Kelly or Kim Novak "out of focus," he also makes especially threatening shots seem to be "behind a veil," "milky," inexact. I mention this for this reason: I heard some time ago that in the face of great anxiety, in a particularly dangerous situation, the frightened person is so upset that he becomes nearsighted. Hitchcock has therefore turned psychic events into an image sentence.

We can say that in the genre films mentioned the image language may have been cultivated early and also numbed into a fixed canon which is unchangeable and yet most flexible. It appears, however, that more and more—and for this reason it concerns me here—the so-called impartial films (we rightly call them problem films or artistic films), which pretend to show quite impartial images, unpleasant, sterile shots, mechanically repeated, which pretend not to describe and to have no normative language, are really biased. These artistic films, while pretending to give back the outer world of filmed objects in images, actually give back only the inner world, the rigidified grammar of film forms. Famous filmmakers like Ingmar Bergman work in this way; also Alain Resnais, who with his last film, *La Guerre est Finie,* and now with *Je t'aime, Je t'aime,* could not even repeat his own efforts, which after *Hiroshima, mon amour* had already been unpleasant enough. The completed grammar of these films turns out to be usable for only the most unpleasant, that is, the *simplest* meaning: that is, for unmitigated trash. Godard's film grammar, too, has become, one could say, "fixed." The sequence of shots which he has developed is so completely adaptable that with its help one can establish a new genre film—not a crime movie, nor a western or a horror movie—a Godard film. The dilemma of film is that its syntax grows harder and harder. The way out of this dilemma seems to be that this syntax should be given some thought, that it should be made conscious with the film, that it should be presented; yes, that the syntax of films should appear so abstract that it itself will be shown as the film. Here we can mention some experiments.

Francois Truffaut's *The Bride Wore Black* seems to me an inoffensive film. The plot is clear ahead of time. The story is not invented, it is found—that is, it is known to the viewer from other films. Here it is only brought forward to him as a *film* story; the formal conclusions are so clear that not a single variation seems possible. When a variation does become possible (in the shot in which the actual murderer of the bridegroom is arrested by the police just before the bride can shoot him), one is disappointed because one takes this occurrence as a reversal in the fiction. Later, of course, everything runs its natural course. What baffles me about Truffaut's film? It seems to me that the director, although he sees more sharply than others, is still too short-sighted; the film dramaturgy is in no way abstract, but is very simply exploited. In this way, surely against the will of the author, the film becomes a near parody, and often the contra*diction* between the idyllic quality of the actual shot and the threatening quality of the entire film reminded me only of the old *Ladykillers*: the idyllic was only comic, a little enervating, perhaps with the giddy atmosphere of an English crime comedy. While the comedy makes the dramaturgy clear, the dramaturgy does not make the film into a comedy. Truffaut's film is not much less inoffensive as a comedy; he lacks Hitchcock's exact sincerity. Even the scene in which Jeanne Moreau seals, airtight, with adhesive tape, the door behind which she has confined one of her victims is, in an irritating way, comic, without really working comically. Of course, the shots *earlier* in the film allow this shot to work like a fairy tale, too.

Other attempts to abstract film to its syntax and then, after the reduction, to show images as examples of the syntax, so that the shot actually makes clear the artfulness of the images, are radical. Jean-Marie Straub's *Chronik der Anna Magdalena Bach* has shown the astounding possibilities of film, coupling the strongest and most precise calculation of shots with the strongest and most precise gracefulness—or better put, this film has proved that the most precise artistry leads to the strongest gracefulness. Similar results have been reached by Klaus Lemke with his first film, *48 Hours to Acapulco*; his second film, *Negresco*, went awry because the images also went awry; that is, they were overdeveloped, and the dialogue was babbled.

Examples of showing the syntax of films as the films themselves seem to be manifest above all in American underground films. *The Illiac Passion,* by George Makropoulos, is constructed so that a series of shots is given in a manner similar to a slide lecture. These shots are not, however, thrown one after another on the screen, but gradually, individually, rhythmically repeated and by the repetition formalized into a sequence of shots. As soon as the sequence is made clear, made *visible* in its rhythm, a strange image is injected into the sequence, foreign to the sequence; this strange image now serves as the image which will be rhythmically repeated in the next shot, in which another new image will also appear, which will be repeated in the next rhythmic film unit, whereupon the viewer, who now grasps the syntax, waits in tension for the strange image of this sequence, and so forth. The enormous *affect*ation of these films *effects* an experience which the viewer also *affects* and in which he, in *effect*, participates. A similar tension in viewing operates in the excellent film *Wavelength*, by Michael Snow, in which for forty-five minutes the camera shows nothing but a scantily furnished room. This film presents itself as *affected*; people and objects are not allowed to act, but instead the materials of the film, the film itself, acts—the lighting changes rhythmically, the colors change, so that we see the buses passing on the street once *outside*, or the house address across the street *outside*; then, however, the window to the outside world goes blank again, and only the *inside* of the room can be seen. In addition, a ghastly note of a pipe rises in the course of the film until it reaches the limits of sound. Shortly before the end of the film, after the camera has turned slowly around to a picture on the wall, the note breaks off. The picture on the wall is exactly the film image: a photograph of the sea, which the viewer observes for some minutes: the screen crackles, it is now so still.

The advances of film continue, to be sure. We consider them political, though at the same time asocial—more asocial than the advances of theatre, of which we have yet to speak. And as in the theatre, the great "problem films"—those which concern themselves with (unfortunately) truly eternal questions—appear as art films. It no longer holds true, as Walter Benjamin claimed, that as a consequence of its technical reproducibility, film has nothing of the ritual artistic aura. This might still have been true in 1930; today, however, it seems that that very technical reproducibility of film has given it the ability to create illusions of the second grade, naive illusions which the theatre no longer achieves today. How often do you hear, for example, people say, who claim to have seen through the theatre's pretensions to Art, that they "prefer to go to the movies, only, of course, when a truly artistic film, a film worth seeing, is playing"? *Blow-Up*, the Bergman films, Fellini films, the films of Godard replace, for such people, the Hamlet-aura which, we understand, they can no longer endure. These films, precisely because they are reproducible and two-dimensional, raise for the public the great questions of being (three-dimensional). It seems that the formal three-dimensionality of the ordinary theatre conflicts with the promoted three-dimensionality of theme. The artistic quality of the flat screen, however, distances and allows the remaining *space* all the big questions. Problem films are the most dishonest genre films because they—in contrast to crime films and so forth—pretend to be so frightfully real and natural because they use the rules of play, but do not make them recognizable: a film about love, a film about suffering, a film about death—each is a genre film. Death, whenever filmed, has rules of play; most of these films do not show that. They have also become edifying experiences; even the cost of admission approximates that of the theatre.

What effect the restrictions of production have, I do not know, nor whether they are more serious in the theatre or in film. Already the costs of production are leading in the direction that the producer, if he wants to continue to produce, must eliminate every radical thought because of economic considerations. The asocially existing social film—the underground film—exists less easily than the asocially existing social theatre. The theatre can afford, in the economic sense, to exist a little asocially; even the small theatre has a position of some importance in the business structure. Underground films, however, have not yet created any such position of importance in business. Not only are they denied publicity; they are also denied publication. The self-proclaimed, as well as the actually, radical theatre, on the other hand, can count at least on world-wide publication if not, in fact, on publicity. The radical film, unfortunately, has been able to produce no public interest. Straub's film can be shown only in Sunday matinees before startled Bach lovers.

Theatre, on the other hand, has publicity. The business system is such that what happens on stage will be discussed in any case. Events of the theatre are, at least, made public. The theatre has a claim to publication from tradition. By a right of custom the theatre has become and remained an indirect means of mass communication. Had it, of course, by its reactionary method of communication forfeited that claim, it would need the administration of the State, and could not rely on so-called diversity of opinion. In this way the theatre has an unearned right to publicity which, however, its promoters earned. We will follow up on that. The administrator should earn this right to publicity! The theatre has a good possibility of squeezing through, because it also likes to be scornful as an institution. The theatre can be craftily employed—with it one can dispossess oneself from merely *private* expressions: one makes himself public. Of course, a blind self-exposure is insignificant in received dramaturgy and more painful than the same blindness in film. But there are examples of the possibility of theatre to display direct—not reproduced—movements, words, and actions, which have an effect only because they are presented live, not reproduced. If they were filmed, they would be artificial in a quite *natural, usual* manner, while in the theatre they operate immediately, directly, spatially. They are *artificially* artificial; they are *in the making* and not *made*. In Paris I recently saw the Bread and Puppet Theatre from New York, which convinced me of the possibilities, not of theatre, but of direct presentation of actions. The traditional dramaturgy, which recognizes only action and words which *serve* the story, is reduced to actions and words, noises and clangs themselves; they become incidents which show nothing else, but present themselves as theatrical events. Actions act themselves and words talk themselves. The viewer, who awaits in the theatre the resolution of every word and every action, the thematic sense, the story, will be left with the action alone. The raising of a hand is a story. Buzzing is a story. Sitting, lying, and standing are stories. A very exciting story is the striking of a hammer against iron. Every word, every sound, every movement is a story: they lead to nothing, they remain visible for themselves alone. Every utterance is *made;* no action results naturally from the preceding action; no utterance means anything other than itself— it signifies itself. An unheard-of simultaneity of sight, breath, and discrimination is created. The space forms a theatrical unity, in which one becomes increasingly self-conscious and tense, almost to the point that the socially protective adhesive tape with which everyone wraps himself is ripped, is no longer visible, not only without, but also within, in the consciousness of the viewer.

This intense artificiality is replaced in the movies by a technical artificiality: here the theatre, as direct presentation, has one possibility *more* than film. The theatre has the possibility of becoming more artificial, and in that way it is endlessly *unusual,* unfamiliar. It can fully utilize the mechanism of the viewer, in order to bring him to confusion. As long as it is that way, I prefer of course to go to the movies. But I less like to write a filmscript than a play. The misery of comparison.

Filmography

SELECTIVE LIST OF FILMS BASED ON PLAYS

The following list of films based on the plays of forty selceted playwrights is derived from A. G. S. Enser, *Filmed Books and Plays* (New York: Seminar Press, 1971), which should be consulted for the most exhaustive listing available. For Shakespeare, see also Robert H. Ball, *Shakespeare on Silent Film* (London: Allen and Unwin, 1968) and Roger Manvell, *Shakespeare and the Film* (New York: Praeger, 1971).

Albee, Edward
  Who's Afraid of Virginia Woolf? (Warner Brothers, 1965)
Anouilh, Jean
  Becket (Paramount, 1963)
  Waltz of the Toreadors (J. Arthur Rank, 1962)
Barrie, James
  Admirable Crichton, The (Columbia, 1957)
  Forever Female (Rosalind) (Paramount, 1953)
  Peter Pan (RKO, 1953)
  Quality Street (RKO, 1937)
  Seven Days Leave (The Old Lady Shows Her Medals) (Paramount, 1930)
  What Every Woman Knows (MGM, 1934)
Behan, Brendon
  Quare Fellow, The (British Lion, 1962)
Bolt, Robert
  Man for All Seasons, A (Columbia, 1968)
Chekhov, Anton
  Seagull, The (Warner Brothers, 1969)
Coward, Noel
  Astonished Heart, The (General Film Distributors, 1949)
  Bittersweet (MGM, 1940)
  Blithe Spirit (Cineguild, 1945)
  Brief Encounter (Still Life) (Cineguild, 1946)

Cavalcade (Twentieth Century Fox, 1933 and 1955)
Design for Living (Paramount, 1933)
Fumed Oak (General Film Distributors, 1952)
Meet Me Tonight (General Film Distributors, 1952)
Pretty Polly (*Pretty Polly Barton*) (J. Arthur Rank, 1967)
Private Lives (MGM, 1931)
Red Peppers (General Film Distributors, 1952)
This Happy Breed (Cineguild, 1944)
Tonight at 8:30 (General Film Distributors, 1952)
Tonight is Ours (*The Queen Was in the Parlor*) (Paramount, 1933)
Ways and Means (General Film Distributors, 1952)
We Were Dancing (MGM, 1942)

Delaney, Shelagh
Taste of Honey, A (British Lion, 1961)

Dürrenmatt, Friedrich
Visit, The (Twentieth Century Fox, 1964)

Eliot, T. S.
Murder in the Cathedral (Film Traders, 1951)

Feydeau, Georges
Flea in Her Ear, A (Twentieth Century Fox, 1968)

Gay, John
Beggar's Opera, The (British Lion, 1953)

Gelber, Jack
Connection, The (Continental Films, 1962)

Genet, Jean
Balcony, The (British Lion, 1963)

Gogol, Nikolai Vasilevich
Inspector General, The (Warner Brothers, 1949)

Hansberry, Lorraine
Raisin in the Sun, A (Columbia, 1960)

Hellman, Lillian
Another Part of the Forest (Universal, 1948)
Little Foxes, The (RKO, 1941)
Loudest Whisper, The (*The Children's Hour*) (United Artists, 1962)
Searching Wind, The (Paramount, 1946)
These Three (*The Children's Hour*) (United Artists, 1936)
Toys in the Attic (United Artists, 1963)
Watch on the Rhine (Warner Brothers, 1943)

Inge, William
Come Back, Little Sheba (Paramount, 1952)

Dark at the Top of the Stairs, The (Warner Brothers, 1960)
Picnic (Columbia, 1955)
Stripper, The (A Loss of Roses) (Twentieth Century Fox, 1963)
Jellicoe, Ann
Knack, The (United Artists, 1965)
Jonson, Ben
Volpone (Siritzky, 1947)
Kopit, Arthur
Oh Dad, Poor Dad (Paramount, 1966)
Marlowe, Christopher
Doctor Faustus (British Lion, 1966, and Columbia, 1968)
Miller, Arthur
Crucible, The (Films de France, 1957)
Death of a Salesman (Columbia, 1951)
View from the Bridge, A (Transcontinental, 1961)
O'Casey, Sean
Juno and the Paycock (British International, 1930)
Plough and the Stars, The (RKO, 1936)
Odets, Clifford
Big Knife, The (United Artists, 1955)
Clash by Night (RKO, 1952)
Country Girl, The (Winter Journey) (Paramount, 1954)
Golden Boy (Columbia, 1938)
O'Neill, Eugene
Ah Wilderness! (MGM, 1935)
Anna Christie (MGM, 1930)
Desire Under the Elms (Paramount, 1958)
Emperor Jones, The (United Artists, 1933)
Hairy Ape, The (United Artists, 1944)
Long Day's Journey into Night (Twentieth Century Fox, 1962)
Long Voyage Home, The (United Artists, 1940)
Mourning Becomes Electra (RKO, 1948)
Strange Interlude (MGM, 1932)
Summer Holiday (Ah Wilderness!) (MGM, 1932)
Osborne, John
Entertainer, The (British Lion, 1960)
Inadmissible Evidence (Paramount, 1968)
Look Back in Anger (Associated British and Pathe Film Distributors, 1959)
Pinter, Harold

    Birthday Party, The (Cinerama, 1968)
    Caretaker, The (British Lion, 1963)
Sartre, Jean-Paul
  Respectful Prostitute, The (Gala, 1955)
Schnitzler, Arthur
  La Ronde (Commercial, 1951, and British Lion, 1964)
Shakespeare, William
  As You Like It (Twentieth Century Fox, 1936)
  Hamlet (Two Cities, 1948, and Columbia, 1969)
  Henry V (Two Cities, 1945)
  Julius Caesar (MGM, 1953 and 1969)
  King Lear (Columbia, 1969)
  Macbeth (Republic, 1951, and British Lion, 1960)
  Midsummer Night's Dream, A (Warner Brothers, 1935, and Eagle, 1966)
  Othello (United Artists, 1956, and Eagle, 1966)
  Richard III (British Lion, 1955)
  Romeo and Juliet (MGM, 1936; General Film Distributors, 1954; Gala, 1956; J. Arthur Rank, 1966; and Paramount, 1968)
  Taming of the Shrew, The (Invicta, 1933, and Columbia, 1968)
  Tempest, The (Rafters, 1969)
  Winter's Tale, The (Warner Brothers, 1968)
Shaw, George Bernard
  Androcles and the Lion (RKO, 1952)
  Arms and the Man (Gaumont British, 1932)
  Caesar and Cleopatra (Pascal, 1945)
  Devil's Disciple, The (United Artists, 1959)
  Doctor's Dilemma, The (MGM, 1958)
  Great Catherine, The (Warner Brothers, 1968)
  Major Barbara (Pascal, 1941)
  Millionairess, The (Twentieth Century Fox, 1960)
  My Fair Lady (Pygmalion) (Warner Brothers, 1964)
  Pygmalion (MGM, 1938)
  Saint Joan (United Artists, 1957)
Sherwood, Robert Emmet
  Abe Lincoln in Illinois (Abe Lincoln of Illinois) (RKO, 1940)
  Escape in the Desert (The Petrified Forest) (Warner Brothers, 1945)
  Gaby (Waterloo Bridge) (MGM, 1955)
  Idiot's Delight (MGM, 1939)
  Jupiter's Darling (The Road to Rome) (MGM, 1954)
  Petrified Forest, The (Warner Brothers, 1936)

Reunion in Vienna (MGM, 1933)
Royal Bed (*The Queen's Husband*) (RKO, 1931)
Two Kinds of Woman (*This is New York*) (Paramount, 1932)
Waterloo Bridge (Universal, 1930, and MGM, 1940)
Simpson, Norman Frederick
One Way Pendulum (United Artists, 1964)
Sophocles
Oedipus Rex (Oedipus Rex, 1956, and J. Arthur Rank, 1968)
Strindberg, August
Dance of Death, The (Paramount, 1969)
Miss Julie (London Films, 1951)
Wesker, Arnold
The Kitchen (British Lion, 1961)
Wilde, Oscar
Ideal Husband, An (British Lion, 1948)
Importance of Being Earnest, The (General Film Distributors, 1952)
Lady Windermere's Fan (Twentieth Century Fox, 1949)
Wilder, Thornton
Matchmaker, The (Paramount, 1958)
Our Town (United Artists, 1940)
Williams, Tennessee
Baby Doll (Warner Brothers, 1956)
Boom! (*The Milk Train Doesn't Stop Here Any More*) (Universal, 1968)
Cat on a Hot Tin Roof (MGM, 1958)
Fugitive Kind, The (*Orpheus Descending*) (United Artists, 1960)
Glass Menagerie, The (Warner Brothers, 1950)
Night of the Iguana, The (MGM, 1963)
Period of Adjustment (MGM, 1962)
Rose Tattoo, The (Paramount, 1954)
Streetcar Named Desire, A (Warner Brothers, 1951)
Suddenly Last Summer (Columbia, 1959)
Summer and Smoke (Paramount, 1962)
Sweet Bird of Youth (MGM, 1962)
This Property is Condemned (Paramount, 1966)

Selected Bibliography

Comparisons of film and theatre are so pervasive that almost any bibliography of film theory and criticism constitutes also a bibliography of film and theatre. The following items have been selected on the same principles as the essays in the anthology, to include a wide range of time, methods, and points of view. For a thorough bibliography of the early criticism, up to 1937, see the bibliography in Allardyce Nicoll, *Film and Theatre*, pp. 195–241. Items marked with an asterisk are included or represented in the text of this volume.

Alpert, Hollis. "Film and Theatre." In *The Dreams and the Dreamers: Adventures of a Professional Movie Goer*, pp. 233–251. New York: Macmillan, 1962. Argues that film is the best form of drama.

Arnheim, Rudolf. *Film as Art*. Berkeley and Los Angeles: University of California Press, 1957. The last essay in this collection, "A New Laocoön: Artistic Composites and the Talking Film" (1938), compares film with theatre, as well as with other arts. In the 1957 edition Arnheim reiterates his belief that "the talking film is a hybrid medium," inferior to the silent film.

Artaud, Antonin. "Scenarios and Arguments." *The Drama Review*, T33 (1966), pp. 166–85. "When this art's exhilaration has been blended in the right proportions, [film] will leave the theatre far behind and we will relegate the latter to the attic of our memories."

Balázs, Béla. *Theory of the Film: Character and Growth of a New Art*. Translated by Edith Bone. New York: Roy Publishers, Inc., 1953. A major Hungarian critic's theoretical observations. Emphasis is on the difference between film and theatre in their use of space, time, and point of view. See especially chapter 3, "A New Form-Language," and chapter 20, "The Script."

Ball, Robert H. *Shakespeare on Silent Film: A Strange Eventful History*. London: George Allen and Unwin, 1968. A detailed, scholarly study.

Bazin, André. "Theatre and Cinema." In *What Is Cinema?*, pp. 76–124. Edited and translated by Hugh Gray. Berkeley and Los Angeles: University of California Press, 1967. A shrewd and iconoclastic reconsideration of "filmed theatre," in which the noted French critic challenges a number of received ideas on the subject and concludes that "there are no plays that cannot be brought to the screen."

*Bentley, Eric. *The Playwright as Thinker,* pp. 8–16. New York: Harcourt, 1946.

Bergman, Ingmar. "Each Film Is My Last," *The Drama Review,* T33 (1966), pp. 94–101. A translation of two speeches in which Bergman not only pithily and aphoristically states his artistic credo but also makes a number of shrewd observations about the relation of film to theatre and other arts.

Blossom, Roberts. "On Filmstage." *The Drama Review,* T33 (1966), pp. 68–73. A brief illustrated essay on the author's experiments in integrating film with live performance.

Braudy, Leo. "The Freedom of Theatre." In *Jean Renoir: The World of His Films,* pp. 65–103. New York: Doubleday, 1972. A brilliant study of theatre as a "principle of vitality" in Renoir's work, as a "refuge of order amid the freedoms of nature."

Brecht, Bertolt, "The Film, the Novel, and Epic Theatre." In *Brecht on Theatre,* pp. 47–50. Edited and translated by John Willett. New York: Hill and Wang, 1964. A selection from Brecht's account of his lawsuit over the making of Pabst's film version of *The Threepenny Opera,* praising the possibilities of film, but calling for its liberation from commercial interests.

Callenbach, Ernest. "The Natural Exchange: From an Interview with Vito Pandolfi." *The Drama Review,* T33 (1966), pp. 137–40. The prominent Italian director discusses the close relationship between film and theatre in Italy.

Carter, Huntly. *The New Spirit in the Russian Theatre 1917–1928.* New York: Brentano's, 1929. Seminal account of interrelationships of Soviet theatre and film in the twenties.

*Cavander, Kenneth. "Interview with Harold Pinter and Clive Donner." In *Behind the Scenes: Theatre and Film Interviews,* pp. 211–22. Edited by Joseph F. McCrindle. New York: Holt, Rinehart and Winston, 1971.

Clair, Rene. "From Theatre to Cinema." In *Reflections on the Cinema,* pp. 107–13. Translated by Vera Traill. London: William Kimber, 1953. A call for cinema as an autonomous art and for its freedom from commercial control.

Costello, Donald P. *The Serpent's Eye: Shaw and the Cinema.* South Bend, Ind.: University of Notre Dame Press, 1965. An account of Shaw's dealings with the movies and of the film versions of his plays. Excellent filmography and bibliography.

Cross, Brenda, ed. *The Film Hamlet: A Record of Its Production*. London: Saturn Press, 1948. A collection of short essays on the making of the film by Olivier and fourteen others associated with it.

Dent, Alan, ed. *Hamlet: The Film and the Play*. London: World Film Publishers, 1948. The screenplay of Olivier's film, with introductory essays by Olivier, Dent (the adaptor), and Roger Furse (the designer).

*Eisenstein, Sergei. *Film Form: Essays in Film Theory*. Edited and translated by Jay Leyda. New York: Harcourt, Brace, and World, 1949.

Foreman, Carl and Tyrone Guthrie. "Debate: Movies versus Theatre." *New York Times Magazine*, April 29, 1962, pp. 10, 11, 43, 45, 46, 48, 50 and 53. Foreman says the theatre is obsolete and has been succeeded by the movies; Guthrie says not.

Frye, Northrop. "Specific Forms of Drama." In *Anatomy of Criticism*, pp. 282–92. New York: Athenaeum, 1965. The most influential modern literary critic places the movies in a sequence of dramatic forms next to the opera and the masque, as "scenically organized drama."

Fulton, A. R. *Motion Pictures: The Development of an Art from Silent Films to the Age of Television*. Norman: University of Oklahoma Press, 1960. See especially chapter 12: "From Play to Film."

Gauteur, Claude. "A Frenzy of Images: An Interview with Roger Planchon." *The Drama Review*, T33 (1966), pp. 133–36. An interview with the prominent French stage director in which he discusses, among other things, his use of film techniques on the stage.

*Gilman, Richard. "About Nothing—with Precision." In *Common and Uncommon Masks*, pp. 30–37. New York: Random House, 1971.

Giraudoux, Jean. Preface to *Le Film de la Duchesse de Langeais*. Paris: Grasset, 1942. A witty comparison of film and theatre and a call for great language in the film.

Gouhier, Henri. "Acteur de théatre et acteur de cinéma." *Revue Internationale de Filmologie* 3 (1952): 143–47. The film actor creates; the stage actor re-creates.

Gray, Paul. "Catching the Rare Moment: An Interview with Vilgot Sjöman." *The Drama Review*, T33 (1966): 102–5. A brief interview in which Sjöman describes his experiences in working with theatre-trained and amateur actors.

———. "Cinéma Verité: An Interview with Barbet Schroeder." T33 (1966), pp. 130–32. An interview with a French filmmaker concerning *cinéma verité* as an escape from theatrical influence.

———. "Class Theatre, Class Film: An Interview with Lindsay Anderson." *The Drama Review*, T33 (1966), pp. 122–29. A discussion of current relationships between film and theatre in Britain.

———. "Growing Apart: From an Interview with Roger Blin." *The Drama Review*, T33 (1966), pp. 115–16. A discussion of film versus theatre in the work of leading French writers, especially Artaud, Beckett, and Genet.

———. "A Living World: An Interview with Peter Weiss." *The Drama Review*, T33 (1966), pp. 106–14. Weiss explains why he stopped making films and began working in the theatre.

———. "One Kind of Film-making: From an Interview with Pavel Hobl." *The Drama Review*, T33 (1966), pp. 150–53. An interview with the prominent Czech film director, concerning the relationship of film and theatre in his own work and in Czechoslovakia in general.

Grotowski, Jerzy. "Towards a Poor Theatre." In *Towards a Poor Theatre*, pp. 15–25. New York: Simon and Schuster, 1969. An attack on the "rich theatre," which tries to compete with movies and television by multiplying assimilated elements and a call for a "poor theatre," which focuses on the essence of the theatre: the actor's confrontation with the audience.

*Handke, Peter. "Theater und Film: Das Elend des Vergleichens." In *Prosa, Gedichte, Theaterstücke, Hörspiel Aufsätze*, pp. 314–26. Frankfurt: Suhrkamp Verlag, 1969.

Johnson, Ian. "Merely Players." *Films and Filming* X (April, 1964), pp. 41–48. About Shakespearean films.

*Kauffmann, Stanley. "Notes on Theater-and-Film." *Performance* I (September–October 1972), pp. 104–9.

*Kazan, Elia. Interview in *Directors at Work: Interviews with American Film-Makers*, pp. 149–73 Interviews conducted and edited by Bernard R. Kantor, Irwin R. Blacker, and Anne Kramer. New York: Funk and Wagnalls, 1970.

Kirby, Michael. "The Uses of Film in the New Theatre," *The Drama Review*, T33 (1966), pp. 49–61. A useful survey of recent experiments in the use of film onstage.

Kracauer, Siegfried. "The Theatrical Story" and "Remarks on the Actor." In *Theory of Film: The Redemption of Physical Reality*, pp. 93–101 and 215–31. New York: Oxford University Press, 1960. Considerations by a major realist film critic of the differing qualities and functions of stage and screen actors and of the differing structures of stage and film narratives.

Lawson, John Howard. "Theatre." In *Film: The Creative Process*, pp. 187–94. New York: Hill and Wang, 1964. "The sense of reality is the key to the response of theatre and film audiences. "

Leech, Clifford. "Dialogue for Stage and Screen." *Penguin Film Review*, no. 6 (1958), pp. 97–103. "Neither the stage-play nor the platform-speech can serve as a model for film dialogue or commentary."

Linden, George. "The Staged World." In *Reflections on the Screen*, pp. 2–29. Belmont, Cal.: Wadsworth, 1970. A lively survey of the major differences between film and theatre, touching on language, structure, audience experience, use of time and space, acting, and illusion.

*Lindsay, Vachel. "Thirty Differences Between the Photoplays and the Stage." In *The Art of the Moving Picture*, pp. 179–98. New York: Liveright, 1916. Reprinted 1970.

MacLiammhoir, Michael. *Put Money in Thy Purse*. London: Methuen, 1952. An account of the making of Welles' *Othello*, by the actor who played Iago.

Manvell, Roger. *Shakespeare and the Film*. New York: Praeger, 1971. A general survey. See also Ball.

Meyerhold, Vsevolod. "Two Lectures on Film." *The Drama Review*, T33 (1966), pp. 186–95. A selection from *Reconstruction of the Theatre* (1930): "The reconstructed theatre, using every technical means at its disposal, will work with film, so that scenes played by the actor on stage can alternate with scenes he has played on screen." Also a lecture on "Chaplin and Chaplinism" (1936).

*Nicoll, Allardyce. *Film and Theatre*. New York: Thomas Y. Crowell, 1937.

Panofsky, Erwin. "Style and Medium in the Motion Pictures." *Critique* I (1947): 5–18 and 27–28. Reprinted in Daniel Talbot, ed. *Film: An Anthology*, pp. 15–32. Berkeley and Los Angeles: University of California Press, 1970. Still one of the best descriptions of the film as a medium, with many of its points made through comparison and contrast with the theatre.

Pudovkin, V. I. *Film Technique* and *Film Acting*. Edited and translated by Ivor Montagu. New York: Grove Press, 1957. First published outside Russia in 1929 and 1933, these books remain classics of film technique. See, especially, "The Peculiarities of Film Material" in *Film Technique* and "The Theatre and the Cinema" in *Film Acting*.

Reeves, Geoffrey. "Finding Shakespeare on Film: From an Interview with Peter Brook." *The Drama Review*, T33 (1966), pp. 117–21. A discussion of modern film techniques that might capture the effect of the bare Elizabethan stage.

*Ross, Lillian, and Helen Ross. *The Player: Profile of An Art*. New York: Simon and Schuster, 1962.

*Shaw, Bernard, and Archibald Henderson. "Drama, the Theatre, and the Films." In *Table-Talk of G.B.S.*, pp. 53–65. New York: Harper, 1925. For Shaw's other writings on the film, see the bibliography to Costello (above).

Shelley, Frank. *Stage and Screen*. London: Pendulum, 1946. A short, rather superficial monograph, but with some interesting anecdotes about English actors and directors.

Sontag, Susan. "Theatre and Film." In *Styles of Radical Will*, pp. 99–122. New York: Farrar, Straus and Giroux, 1960. Originally published in *The Drama Review* special issue on film and theatre in 1966, this brilliant and comprehensive essay is particularly enriched by Miss Sontag's insight into recent forms of both film and theatre.

Souriau, Étienne. "Filmologie et esthétique comparée." *Revue internationale de filmologie* 3 (1952): 113–41. A leading French aesthetician considers the relation of film to theatre, as well as to other arts.

Svoboda, Josef. "Laterna Magika." *The Drama Review*, T33 (1966), pp. 141–49. A description of the work of the Czechoslovakian company, in which "film, theatre, and the dialogue between the two media are used as equal components."

Vardac, A. Nicholas. *From Stage to Screen: Theatrical Method from Garrick to Griffith*. Cambridge, Mass.: Harvard University Press, 1949. Traces the vogue of romantic-realistic melodrama through the nineteenth century and shows how the early film was a logical extension of the style.

Virmaux, Alain. "Artaud and the Film." *The Drama Review*, T33 (1966), pp. 154–65. "A complete re-evaluation of Artaud's contribution to film and its place in his writings."

*Von Sternberg, Josef. "Acting in Film and Theatre." *Film Culture* I, no. 5–6 (1955), pp. 1–4, 27–29.

Wilder, Thornton. *"Our Town*—From Stage to Screen: A Correspondence Between Thornton Wilder and Sol Lesser." *Theatre Arts* XXIV (November 1940), pp. 815–24. "An illuminating insight both personal and technical into the translation of an excellent play into an excellent motion picture."

Williams, Raymond, and Michael Orrom. *Preface to Film*. London: Film Drama, 1954. Williams argues the film is essentially an extension of theatre; Orrom calls for a film technique that exploits fully the expressive powers of all the arts it presumably incorporates.

Wollen, Peter. "Eisenstein's Aesthetics." In *Signs and Meaning in the Cinema*, pp. 19–70. Bloomington, Ind.: Indiana University Press, 1972. Discusses, among other things, the influence of the theatre upon Eisenstein's ideas and practice.

Youngblood, Gene. "Intermedia Theatre." In *Expanded Cinema*, pp. 365–86. New York: E. P. Dutton, 1970. Pictures and descriptions of the work of Carolee Schneemann, Milton Cohen, John Cage and Ron Nameth, Robert Whitman, Aldo Tambellini, and Wolf Vostell, all of whom have combined film and live theatre in various ways.

Index